# RECOLLECTIONS OF A JOURNALIST

## A COLLECTION OF PERSONAL STORIES FROM INTERVIEWS

# JACK BEHRENS

Recollections of a Journalist
A Collection of Personal Stories From Interviews
All Rights Reserved.
Copyright © 2018 Jack Behrens
v1.0

The opinions expressed in this manuscript are solely the opinions of the author and do not represent the opinions or thoughts of the publisher. The author has represented and warranted full ownership and/or legal right to publish all the materials in this book.

This book may not be reproduced, transmitted, or stored in whole or in part by any means, including graphic, electronic, or mechanical without the express written consent of the publisher except in the case of brief quotations embodied in critical articles and reviews.

Jack Behrens Publishing
For information visit: www.writerjackweb.com

ISBN: 978-0-578-20243-3

Library of Congress Control Number: 2018937796

Graphics and production were prepared by Lisi Design, Holland Patent, NY

PRINTED IN THE UNITED STATES OF AMERICA

# TABLE OF CONTENTS

### INTRODUCTION
Gertrude Nolte Middlebrook Behrens *7*

### ALEX HALEY
God's Story tellers *13*

### VAUGHN MONROE
WWII vocal heart throb *23*

### WOODY HERMAN
And his new thundering herd *31*

### SYNGMAN RHEE
President of South Korea • 1946-1960 *37*

### BOB HOPE
The eternal wise cracker *45*

### BILL SANDERS
An award-winning cartoonist at Stars & Stripes *51*

### DUKE ELLINGTON
Interviewing Duke Ellington *59*

### WALT DISNEY
A Giant Among Geniuses *65*

### TOM CLANCY
An imaginative military writer *71*

### JOHN SLADE
Teacher, Philosopher, Author *77*

# PHOTO CREDITS

US Army Signal Corps, Front Cover Pvt. John "Jack" Behrens, Combat, Recon Photographer, US Army

Photo of Alex Haley, Utica College

Photos of President Jimmy Carter (Courtesy of Jimmy Carter Library)

Photos of the Doobie Brothers, by Gert Behrens

Photo of Ringling Brothers Barnum Bailey Circus Clown Happy Harry Sinclair courtesy Accent t on Living Magazine

Photo of Vaughn Monroe by Lake Breeze Pier Ballroom, Buckeye Lake, OH

Front Cover of John Behrens (courtesy of Signal Corps, Fort Monmouth, NJ)

Chip Davis (courtesy of American Gramophone - Scott Dobry)

Photo of Alex Haley at Utica College (UC Photos)

Photo of Jack Behrens & at Eastman Theater, Rochester, NY (courtesy of Mark Behren

Photo of Bill Sanders (courtesy of Wikipedia)

Photos of President Ronald Reagan (courtesy of Ronald Reagan Library)

Photo of Vaughn Monroe (courtesy of Wikipedia)

Photo of Tom Clancy (courtesy of Wikipedia)

Photo of Vaughn Monroe (courtesy of the Vaughn Monroe Society)

Photo of President Lyndon Baines Johnson (Library Audiovisual Archives)

Photo of Doobie Brothers by Gert Behrens

Photo President Jimmy Carter (Jimmy Carter Library)

Photo of Jack & Gertrude (Jason Koerner Photography)

Photo of Walt Disney by Marshal Space Flight Center of the US NASA

Gary Wayne Gilbert

# ACKNOWLEDGEMENTS

Kathy Randall, Media Center, UC student Bill Randall

# Table of Contents

### JAMES MICHENER
A Meticulous Best-Selling Author *83*

### JESSICA MITFORD
Dying in America is Expensive *91*

### AL NEUHARTH
The man who built Gannett newspapers *97*

### JIMMY CARTER
A different kind of White House *105*

### LYNDON B. JOHNSON
He excited young voters *115*

### BILL CLINTON
Like all presidents, likeable Bill Clinton was flawed *127*

### RONALD REAGAN
Meeting the President for Lunch *135*

### MR CLOWN
God Bless You, Mr. Clown *143*

### CHIP DAVIS
Was told too many times it couldn't be done *149*

### DOOBIE BROTHERS
The best of the Doobies: what a night! *155*

### TIM CONWAY
Great run as a comic *161*

### EPILOGUE
How did I create my 23rd or 24th book? *169*

# INTRODUCTION
## ★★★★★
## Gertrude Nolte Middlebrook Behrens

I am a Christian and the wife of Jack Behrens. I would like to tell you how God inspired Jack to write this book and the people who encouraged Jack along the way.

Jack and I married six years ago. I am a Nurse (RN) Psychotherapist with a cardiac specialty. One year after we married, Jack was diagnosed with Parkinson's disease. About three years into marriage, he had progressed in the disease to the point where he had to give up writing (he couldn't even write his name), and was pretty much wheelchair bound and depressed. My grandson, Eoin, and his girl-

## INTRODUCTION

friend, Meghan Schauster, both history buffs, were visiting and Jack gave them permission to go through his files.

*Family assistants Meghan Schauster, Eoin Middlebrook and my wife Gert*

At the end of a long afternoon, Eoin came out and told my husband he had found a treasure trove "of stuff on Alex Haley," a longtime friend of Jack's, and he would even organize what he found so that Jack, a writer and professor of US history and journalism, could write another book. This seemed to excite Jack.

My husband has also developed what is known as Parkinson's dementia. This type is a little different than other types of dementia in how it affects the brain. In Jack's case, he can't remember much of anything that happens in the present. His past recollections, however, are extremely sharp which allows him to recall incidents and episodes as though they occurred yesterday.

Enter Dr. Paul Schmidt his neurologist. Jack went for his checkup and told the doctor the drug he was taking did not seem to help him. Dr. Schmidt said he would like Jack to try a new drug , experimental at the time.

Since Jack's been on the drug, he is walking again with a walker for balance, using his hands to type on the computer and writing again. He surprised me and a good number of people at my birthday party by getting up on his own and dancing with me. Not shuffling. . .dancing!

## INTRODUCTION

His incredible recall has brought about the chapters in this book from a past that reaches back more than 60 years. Jack has had great flashbacks; he woke up one morning and said he could smell Korea.

Jack has had a great deal of joy and fun remembering people, circumstances and times. Our evening meals have been exciting for me as I listen to stories about people like Tim Conway and his antics while in the service with Jack in Korea. Ronald Reagan, one of my favorite presidents, invited Jack to the White House. Later, Jack had the opportunity to go to Camp David. He wrote about the presidents' use of the camp in the book Camp David. He also writes about his good friend and fellow writer Alex Haley and how they helped each other. His story about Bob Hope and his favorite organization, the USO, tells why he's a strong supporter for those in the military.

Other members

*Jack's photo inside the old Korean capitol building looking out from a shell cratered wall just after the Korean War Armistice* Jack Behrens's Photo

*Gertrude's daughter Joy Karnes Limoge*

*Jack's daughter Cindy Daugherty*

## INTRODUCTION

of our two families have given support and help in this effort. His daughter Cynthia Daugherty, and my daughter Joy Karnes Limoge, his son Mark Behrens and my son Robert Middlebrook have helped him realize a dream come true with this book. You'll see why others have said he was not only a good teacher, he was a good reporter and writer. This book has been exciting to me as it helped Jack to share his personality, experience and interactions with people. It allows you, the reader to see this wonderful man I married and why I call him "my Prince Charming."

Gertrude Nolte Middlebrook Behrens

*Jack and his son Mark Behrens*

# ALEX HALEY
## ★★★★★
### God's Story Teller

Playboy writer and author Alex Haley of "Roots" and I had a great 20 year relationship that started when I got a call from a friend at Hamilton College in Clinton, NY. It was 1966-67. Alex had accepted a writer-in-residence contract from Hamilton probably through his agent. He was looking for some idea of what to expect in classes at an affluent and rural liberal arts college.

We met within a few days at the Student Union at Utica College where I had been teaching journalism courses for about four years fresh out of the service and one year at Ohio Wesleyan University in Delaware, OH.

I loved teaching magazine writing and I was anxious for Alex to feel what I meant. He said he felt that the day we chatted. I had read some of his pieces in Playboy. I recall that I had to hide the magazine from my wife because of the cover and the content. She saw it on the couch one day and told me that "you have a daughter and do you want her to see that type of garbage in this house?" I could tell she was upset. Her attitude bordered on rage and some curiosity. "Isn't our sex life enough for you?" she demanded. I did the sputtering male defense of what I knew was true. I'm a writer, I said, and this is a magazine that is one of the top in the field of non-fiction today. I teach the subject. Am I to avoid it because it sells sex on the cover?

Not good enough for Patty and she told me so. Okay, I said, it will be in my office only and I'll make sure I close the door.

When Alex and I met that next day, we sat down and had three cups of coffee for four hours straight, that started our relationship. We both enjoyed one another for two decades on the phone, at his small place in Clinton, my office, and by mail.

His first question after pleasantries was "Exactly what is a syllabus? The dean said I have to put one together." I told him it means planning out probably 13 or more weeks of classes and what you would discuss in each. I can help with that based on what you want to accomplish and what you want students to do, I replied.

He sighed. "Does it have to be that explicit? I thought I could just talk about how I do what I do and try to offer examples along the way, wouldn't that suffice?" Yes and no, I

*Alex Haley & Jack at Utica College*  Utica College

answered pausing to see if he understood what I meant. "You realize that you're talking to an audience of beginning 18 to 20 year olds with one thing in mind: what am I going to have do in this class for an hour and how much will I have to do to get a good grade?"

"Wouldn't they be interested in such kind of work?" he questioned me. "Not until they know what they have to do, Alex," I told him. His face turned ashen. He didn't say anything for a couple of minutes.

*Alex Haley at Utica College*
Utica College

"Teaching is much more then telling stories, Alex, trust me," I explained as nicely as I could. He smiled and sat back and drank more coffee.

"My Hamilton contact said that I would have grading to do but I guess I didn't expect being tied up for several months at a time," he retorted still thinking about what this would entail. "You need to think about your time first especially if you are planning a major block away from campus because that would probably be difficult for the college to accommodate," I answered.

"Thanks for being honest with me, John, that helps," he said and then added that we should get together "often." He asked for several copies of what I used in my classes and then we finished by talking about his family and some of his friends.

A week or so later he called and asked if we could meet again. We did. This time he brought some of his stories and asked me to read them and let him know if they would be the type of material that could be interesting to a group of "kids." He began by telling about an assignment he got from Playboy to do a profile of Bishop James Pike, a major religious figure in the '60s.

"I decided index cards with questions on each was the best," Alex started. "So I put questions on the cards and then shuffled them in the best order I could think of for when I met the man. I put them aside. I went back to them in a day or two. I had learned that when the idea and questions begin to flow in your mind you need to give yourself space. You cull the questions to no more than 10. I always soften people for the tough ones I knew I had to ask. Easy questions that I knew were feel good types were best to lead off with. Especially for a man who had just lost his son to suicide.

*"To John Behrens - the second journalism professor I ever met."*

He was sitting by his pool in Santa Barbara when I went to meet with the pastor. I surmised from the sweat on his brow in the bright California sun it was going to be different. He was hunched over. Do I use tape recorder or pen and pad? I took a hunch and decided on tape recorder.

When I got to him, he motioned for me to sit. On impulse, I said that I was out of cigarettes but asked him if I could leave the recorder on beside him so he could begin by telling me how he felt while I was gone? I had never done that before but I thought it was worth a try. Bishop Pike shook his head in the affirmative. Occasionally you instinctively feel that some persons aren't open to talking out loud about personal details of their lives. I had this feeling the bishop fit such an MO. Bullseye!"

Alex said he slowly left and walked toward his car a distance away. He said he glanced back every few steps. Sure enough, he said, he could hear the bishop talking to the recorder. "I didn't need to see tears, I could tell the way he was working through his thoughts as the California sun drenched us both," the experienced interviewer explained.

"It was an emotional 75 minutes of a person feeling into himself," Alex added. "it was the kind of thing that came from his being....not his intellect. In doing the story, I used his mood to guide me. It made the whole difference in one of my best stories." And, he added with a smile, "I wasn't even there."

We talked about all kinds of scenarios he had used.

Every interview took as much preparation to get into as it did to write the 2500 or more words in the actual story. Here's an example: "I was asked to interview Melvin Belli, a major defense lawyer with great success in winning legal cases on both coasts. I was told to go to his office and do a full interview with him. I knew that this would require as much as several days at the least. Obviously, I didn't know him. I talked to one of his clients to get a feel for his personality. Depends on his day, I was told. I wouldn't try him on a Monday or Tuesday. Bad days, the client responded.

But he said, 'he loves to find new ways to cook eggs in the mountains! That's a good way to get him going,'" the client told Alex.

"I spent a week finding out all the ways that eggs could be cooked in the mountains and elsewhere," Alex continued smiling. He didn't have Google to get instant information.

"I used more than 4 reels of tape for that interview and caused Melvin to miss an interview with a client too. He was still trying to add more details when I left about five hours later! It was a terrific piece that came from four days of work on the coast and a break from the frigid East Coast weather," the soft-spoken interviewer noted. Food, for some reason, can be a great introduction for a writer. He told how he got the late UN Ambassador Adlai Stevenson to tell him about his love of tomatoes. "I could have written a book from that discussion," he laughed.

He spun another totally different account of a piece he did after he talking to the late Sammy Davis Jr. The singer was loudly bantering outside his dressing room at the Las Vegas hotel with busboys and some musicians.

I stood back from the group, Haley said, but then walked away acting disgusted. I started shuffling though my papers and in an instance, Sammy was walking toward me. "Did you want something?" the singer/dancer asked so that all could hear. "Are you from one of those Black publications in Hollywood?"

"No I'm actually on assignment from Playboy," Alex replied nonchalantly. Davis was obviously interested. "Let's go someplace quiet," the singer responded. Sammy was obviously annoyed. Why wasn't I alerted that a Playboy interviewer was looking for me? Alex said he murmured to himself matter of factly, Davis was upset. "But I know who are you." The singer quipped. "Let's get on with it, okay?"

Alex agreed and for the next several hours he got a good tape from the very popular scat man himself.

How did he get started as a writer? "I didn't intend to be a writer. I wanted to be a cook," he smiled. He joined the US Coast Guard after he dropped out of school and began writing letters to his father who was a professor. "He wanted me to be brilliant and a professor, too," he told me. On board coast guard cutters he became known "as the prolific letter writer." His sailor friends thought that he could help them with their girlfriends. "It started with letters to help out a friend. Then it mushroomed," he said. "I was making a $1 a letter and I soon was making more than I made as a cook," he laughed.

Alex was buried, the Associated Press reported, a few paces from the front porch where he listened as a child to family stories that inspired him to seek his roots. "He made great-grandfathers superstars," said Rev Jesse Jackson. African drums sounded during the burial and a military honor guard was present. The funeral service was held in the church he attended as a small child, The Greenwood Christian Methodist Episcopal Church, in Henning, TN. The former Education Secretary Lamar Alexander, a Tennessean, said it best perhaps. "Alex Haley was God's instrument .. he was God's storyteller."

Fame and celebrity never changed Alex. Said Atha Campbell of Henning at Alex's funeral: "He treated everybody like they were somebody. He didn't ever meet any little folks or big folks. He just met folks."

But fame brings more distasteful repercussions too. The claims against his estate included his third wife Myran Haley of Los Angeles for ownership of three unfinished works, longtime friend and associate Arthur Sims, an $18,750 African mahogany casket with a $2,500 copper liner, insurance agencies, a furniture supply house and banks.

A trust was arranged for his children Lydia and William of his first wife Nannie Virginia Branche and another daughter Cynthia Haley who he had by his second wife Juliette. The will, 20 pages long, said that the children were to be cared for by the residue of the estate.

His death certificate named his first wife Nannie as the surviving spouse.

Alex bought a 127-acre farm in Norris in 1986. He loved the place he told me and he spent nearly $1 million renovating and adding five buildings and a gazebo in the middle of a two-acre lake. He had a staff of five to six to maintain his farm.

The last time I talked to him he told me being a writer was beginning to "cost me money. It seems there is never enough," he said smiling. He told me he had $3 million in the bank. That sounded like a lot in those days. Another friend told me and later the media confirmed that "Alex was generous to a fault."

He supported people who exploited him but he would reply "I know this hurts me but we must think of them and their families too."

At my daughter's graduation from Utica College, he flew in from Los Angeles although he had three engagements on the West Coast within the same week. "I know what this means to you and what are friends for? And she's a Cynthia like my daughter," he said with a grin.

We both agreed to put up $500 for the beginning of an Alex Haley Writing Award at UC.

Examples of Alex's thoughts on subjects:

To students at Unv Of Tennessee: "I think what it really comes down to is people all over the world are hungry for human care, for human concern for human belief and see all of us as people and their potential to have decent lives."

On race relations: "I'm sick of hearing about race relations. I think we are permitting ourselves to be distracted from something far more worrisome. The slow destruction of our planet. All races are a part of the poisoning process . . . Racial hatred has been with man since he first crawled out of caves. It exists everywhere"

*The Beverly Hills Hotel*
AND BUNGALOWS
BEVERLY HILLS · CALIFORNIA

Dear Dr. Donahue:

The other evening, I much enjoyed being a part of the gathering for faculty authors.

And along with this, I've intended several times to express to you that I travel a considerable lot, including a number of colleges and universities, where almost always I'm asked to observe and speak to writing classes -- and I really honestly have been impressed that I've not witnessed a single magazine writing class that I consider as effectively taught as is John Behrens' class there at Utica College. I suppose what immediately prompts this note tonight is that I had just that reflection this afternoon, after seeing how a course of this type is taught here at UCLA. The point is that John focusses his students toward actually selling something. And I know, as a professional writer, how that is more important to the motivation of the writing aspirant than all the theories in the world! I really feel that I would have been maybe two years ahead if, in the beginning, I had been exposed to such a pragmatic approach class as John conducts.

The best wishes to you, and to Mrs. Donahue, and thank you again for inviting me.

Yours sincerely,

*Alex Haley*

Dr. J. Kenneth Donahue

*Alex Haley commenting on Jack Behrens Class at Utica College*

# Vaughn Monroe

## WWII vocal heart throb

His interest in engineering vanished when he won a local trumpet contest. He told his fiancé minutes later at their senior prom that he felt he could support their future as a trumpet player.

Vaughn Monroe, weeks before, had been voted by his Jeanette High School, PA classmates the most likely to succeed. What a way to launch his future as the Great Depression began a few months later in 1930.

He had confidence in himself ... and so did his wife-to-be. In today's security-conscious world that would seem to be suicide. Even in those care free days before the stock market collapsed, it was a big gamble.

He dropped the trumpet and counted on his looks and his rich deep voice to become a very popular singer-bandleader of the 1940s and '50s..

## VAUGHN MONROE

"He was the exception ... a bandleader who, in the public perception, was first and foremost a singer," said Edward Chase on the singer's web page.

And he did it with a marvelous baritone voice and some great arrangements. Vaughn Monroe was an Ohioan. From Akron OH, he grew up along with Tiny Bradshaw, The Edsels, Maureen McGovern, Ron Bell and others in popular music in the Buckeye state. He made his mark with hits like "Let It Snow! Let It Snow! Let It Snow!," "Riders in the Sky," "Ballerina," "There! I've Said It Again" and a good number of large hits from shows of the time.

His theme song "Racing with the Moon" became a hit as did he over the WWII years and a few years afterward. A good looking, 6'2" man he was also well educated at a time when many in the business weren't. Vaughn had a bachelor's from Carnegie Mellon, Carnegie Institute of Technology and the New England Conservatory of Music.

I met him at Buckeye Lake, OH where he squeezed most of his band (14 players and four singers called "The Moon Maids" on a small ballroom platform at the wooden Pier Ballroom which was built over part of the muddy bottomed lake. The ballroom was filled and many were dancing outside while a worried fire marshal watched.

He told me he liked to sing but didn't think his voice would get him the work the trumpet might.

"In those days (1930-1940s) there were a number of good male singers out front of bands like Tommy Dorsey, Artie Shaw, Jimmy and Tommy Dorsey and Harry James just to name a few," he told me. He remembered his dates in Central Ohio which were carried by NBC radio. He said that he was fortunate enough to get a break because most big bands at the time were led by musicians.

I've not forgotten that when I talked with him he told that the Moon Maids, lovely Texas girl backup singers, babysat for members of his orchestra and rarely got introduced at performances. I asked why and he said because they wanted anonymity. They liked touring and singing backup; they didn't want anything more.

"As a singer I was different and it gave me a chance to showcase my voice and band," he said. "And lots of radio time in places like Buckeye Lake, the Meadowbrook as well as Chicago spots like the Aragon put us in a good position. I had signed on Jan Savett's arranger and that paid dividends too. Can you imagine a guy who started out learning to play a bugle would move so far and rise so fast in such a crazy business? That's what happened," he explained.

Wikipedia Photo

Not exactly. A good friend, Jack Marshard, a society bandleader, gave him an ultimatum when he returned from a tour of Ohio, Boston, Colorado, Texas, Kentucky and then back to Boston to the Terrace Gables, Falmouth, MA. Vaughn thought it looked like paradise and wanted to settle down. He was playing trumpet, singing and enjoying his life. But Jack was unhappy and so were some members of his band. Enter band booker and organizer Willard Alexander. He convinced Vaughn to sing and lead his orchestra, put a new one together and move on. Vaughn promptly got in his car and drove straight through to New York City and met Marion. They took a train to Jeanette, married and went to Siler's Ten Acres in New England where he and the band opened on April 10, 1940, the same year that Lionel Hampton, Charlie Spivak, crooner Russ Carlyle, pianist Teddy Powell and a bunch of talented musicians decided to become bandleaders.

His two big hits happened "There! I've Said It Again" and "Let it Snow! Let It Snow! Let It Snow!" His look—6'2" a good looking face, figure and smile—and demeanor made him a natural for Hollywood. He did a number of B films, western, generally. None rose beyond the second flick on a Saturday double feature. "Remember, I was city-dweller. I laughed when I saw myself in boots and on a horse. It wasn't me," he mused.

A few of his musical hits made it to the top of the Hit Parade and his band, which had some journeymen musicians, was named the top college band in the country. He disbanded his orchestra in the early 1950s. He worked in television and on radio, hosting Camel Caravan for many years, and he became a spokesman for RCA Victor. He sold Camel cigarettes and RCA television sets into the 1960s.

*Vaughn Monroe, left, popular bandleader in the 1940s -1960s on a very crowded stage at the Lake Breeze Pier Ballroom, Buckeye Lake, OH during a Camel Caravan radio program*
Courtesy of the Vaughn Monroe Society

Sometime before or after I interviewed him there was speculation that he was offered the Christmas song "Rudolph the Red-nosed

Reindeer" to record. He turned it down it was reported. Gene Autry made it a huge hit. Vaughn recorded "Mule Train" which was used in one of his early films. He was slow to promote it and Frankie Laine made it a big hit later. "I didn't always jump when I should have. My best recording was 'Ballerina' without a doubt," he told me.

We talked about places he played and I mentioned what I saw at Buckeye Lake when the risers were tilting and appeared ready to buckle. "You should have seen me at the Paramount in New York on a Saturday morning show. Big crowd gathered that day. We had to come up on a lift from the basement and when we got to crowd level some teenagers got on to the stage and the kids started getting on top of us. I had two girls tugging at my bow tie—one on each end—and it took stagehands to get them to let go. I lost the tie but saved my skin," he laughed.

I also remembered it because in addition to the band on the platform (shown) were two sound men who were standing precariously on the outside ledge of a riser that didn't look like it would hold the group. Everybody in the audience became fixated on when it would collapse. It didn't.

They finished the show without incident or injuries.
His early days included offers from other bands to join them but he decided he could do it himself. He had a voice to become another Walter Cronkite on television had he gone into announcing but he chose to stick with the band work. "I liked the hours," he joked. "I also enjoyed the interplay with fans around the country." He pointed out that he was strong enough on the horn "that if my voice failed, I could get a job playing again with somebody…somewhere." He never had to.

The Monroe family started in Akron, OH, moved to Cudahy, WI and from there to Jeanette, PA where he met and married his wife

Marian (Baughman). How did he become a trumpet player? According to his parents, one day he came home with it telling them that "the kid down the block gave it to me. He can't play it on account of his teeth." In 1944, he picked up a trombone after a lengthy search and then taught himself how to play and started playing in the 'bone' section of his orchestra as well as singing.

His hobbies took him in different directions. He loved golf, photography, motorcycling, miniature trains, carpentry, swimming, and flying. He frequently sought one-nighters within 300 miles from his residence so he'd get home to be with his wife and their two daughters; Candace and Christina.

He usually would do 100 one-nighters a year. "Flying to them gave me more time for business and it broke up the monotony that I found on the road," he explained to me. It had it's dangers though. One night returning home he was blown off course about 50 miles and landed in a Pennsylvania cabbage patch. "The first night I was late getting home," he told me laughing.

He was admired by a number, mocked by others for his singing and occasional pompous attitude. I remembered him to be very down to earth for a celebrity. Likeable, easy going and approachable. That was the Vaughn Monroe I met and interviewed when the 1950s became the 1960s.

He died in Stuart, FL not far from where I live today.

# Woody Herman
## And his new thundering herd

The crowd of young people and dancers were listening and dancing at the Steel Pier Marine Ballroom in Atlantic City to the exciting music of one of the legendary jazz bands of the century.

Woody Herman and his Thundering New Herd (it replaced four other herds of musicians over the 1940s, 50s, 60s and into 80s) who loved to swing.

And every Herman concert or dance was about the same. Swinging beat, throaty solos from some of the youngest and best players in the business. He was asked once about the key to his success: "Young musicians with great vitality and a love for swing music," he smiled. "If it doesn't swing we have trouble playing it." I loved the way he would find ways to introduce band members. Some leaders refuse to recognize sidemen. Woody did it with gusto. "On bass tonight is a well known patriot, John Adams. They were swinging cats in those days, too," he laughed.

It started when the Milwaukee, WI native graduated from high school and joined a few bands that played ballads and ragtime music at the time. He played with the Harry Sosnick Band. He worked as a singer and tap-dancer thanks to his father Otto who played around the Milwaukee area.

Woody met an aspiring actress, Charlotte Neste, and the two married in 1936. She was an inspiration to him, he once said. She enjoyed music and she didn't mind traveling. For Woodrow Charles Herman, she exceeded his requirements. In the late '30s, the alto saxophonist/clarinetist got a chance with the Gus Arnheim and Isham Jones band where he sang and recorded several numbers that struck paydirt with the band. "Lonesome Me" and "My Heart's at Ease" made Woody a band singer as well as a clarinetist.

Isham was a song writer and wanted to live on his residuals and get off the road. As a result, the band broke up. Woody, meanwhile, saw a chance to form his own group with some of the musicians he was playing with. They formed what was called a collective band and he became the leader.

The band became the Herman band, after Jones retired and it took the name "The Band That Plays the Blues." The name stuck. Decca Record company recorded the first song, "Wintertime Dreams" in November that year and George R. Simon, who wrote for Metronome Magazine, reviewed the band and later wrote: "This Herman outfit bears watching: not only because it's fun listening to in its present stages, but also because it's bound to reach even greater stages." Three years later, the band recorded it's first major hit, "Woodchopper's Ball." That's all Woody needed. It eventually sold more than five million copies.

His Herds, whether numbered or thundering, contained excellent sidemen young and old. I remember people like Chubby Jackson, the happiest and most energetic bassist I'd ever watched; Vito Musso, the Italian tenor saxophonist, who couldn't read but could solo wildly for 15 minutes or more; and later younger Herdsmen like Frank Tiberi, who play nearly any wood instrument available, trumperters such as brothers Pete and Conte Candoli, who were the best in the business in my day in the 50s and later years, Mark Lewis and Don Down.

1980 -Photo Courtiesy of Woody Herman Orchestra

Woody signed on the best for his yearly tours and he looked for young talent especially. That's probably why he picked up the title 'Road Father." "To play our book," he told me that night at the Steel Pier, "you need energy...lotsa energy." He dealt with his share of addicted players but he held fast to his rule; better be ready to play the gig...or else.

His biggest mistake with the band? "Not signing a beautiful southern gal who had a great voice. Her name? Dinah Shore." Years later Dinah and Woody met up at the Tropicana and she asked Woody why it didn't work out. Woody told her that several members of the band wanted a scat singer. "Would you believe that we went with Anita O'Day instead? This is a business of hunches and impulses," he laughed.

Herman had fond memories of the Chicago ballroom the Aragon. "That was quite a place. The first time I went in I nearly got lost in the men's room! The bathrooms had valets and I couldn't get over the space. More than 80,000 square feet of dancing space on the south side of the city. One of the guys playing with us at the time was from Chicago and told us that it was called the 'uptown' because it was near the well-known 'L' of the city's elevated railway," Woody said. "I've been there," I told him. He remarked that "it was the most decorated place to dance I'd seen! To a kid from Milwaukee, it was like a ballroom in the desert... like being in Morocco. Spanish architecture shaped like a palace courtyard. The huge dance floor rested on cork, felt and springs. Man, you certainly knew you were uptown!" he recalled with a grin.

There was an excitement at a Herman dance that was not always seen at others. He generated excitement himself and his sidemen and singers showed the same. It was a celebration of fun, I felt. Dancing was the reason for everybody to be there and Woody made sure that he gave you his best.

At a time when polls were valuable but less scientific, the Herman band was voted the best by Down Beat, Metronome, Billboard, and Esquire. Woody was among a number of musicians such as Duke Ellington, Elliott Lawrence, Benny Goodman and others regarding the commingling of popular music and classical, Woody wrote a celebrated classical piece called "The Ebony Concerto" that many thought raised the bar. He said that the composition was "a very delicate and a very sad piece."

The Ebony Concerto was performed on March 25, 1946, in Carnegie Hall at the zenith of the band's most financially successful year. Months later, the success began to erode and he took some time off. The family had purchased and moved into the Hollywood home of Humphrey Bogart and Lauren Bacall. But, the financial success evaporated as wife's Charlotte's problems with alcoholism and addiction to pills got worse and he disbanded his band.

It was difficult for the longtime leader and friends. Many tried to offer help but the bills continued to mount. He did get Charlotte into AA and she did give up dependence on alcohol and drugs and she tried to help herself.

Woody handled it in stride. He told a reporter that he went to "an AA meeting with Charlotte and found my old band was sitting there." He continued to perform after his wife died, at the same time, his own health declined. But he never stopped looking for new young talent. He formed another group and added people like trombonist Phil Wilson, tenor saxophonist Sal Nistico, trumpeters Bill Chase and Paul Fontaine and drummer Jake Hanna. The band rolled with the times adding rock'n'roll to its itiniery.

But more bad news landed on top of everything else; he owed the IRS millions because of his business manager's mistakes back in the 1960s. Players couldn't get over the fact that Woody continued to pull his old chart of "Things Ain't What They Used To Be" quite often.

*Woody Herman Poster for his first performance at the Roseland Ballroom* Jack Behrens's Image

He was well loved by virtually everyone in the

business and he kept a great sense of humor throughout his tumultuous life. When I talked to him at the Steel Pier that night I asked him how he felt?

"I'm getting too old for this," he sighed, and added "but I still get a kick out of playing and being with young lads with talent. It's a gas!"

Even more important, he could remember how and where he started; the Roseland Ballroom, a former ice skating rink on West 52nd Street in New York City. In 2013, Lady Gaga sold out the final performance at the historic ballroom.

"When your marqee comes down, you know you finished the gig," he smiled. A great number of us from the 1940s, 1950s and through the 1980s still remember the little man with the clarinet who taught us the blues with rhythm.

# SYNGMAN RHEE
## ★★★★★
## President of South Korea • 1946-1960

I interviewed President Syngman Rhee and his wife Franziaka (who translated for him although he spoke and understood English) at the presidential palace in Seoul, Korea in September, 1957.

We talked about his thesis at Princeton on neutrality as an issue in the US when he earned his PhD in 1910. The US, as a free nation, had retained its neutrality for a period of time before WW II but, he said, he realized the need to fight a common foe like the US did in 1941. He talked with me about the division within political parties in the US to join the allies overseas prior to December, 1941 and he said that's what resonated with him when the North Koreans invaded the South.

He was an ardent anti-Communist and in fact that's why he left his native Haeju, North Korea. He fled the north in the 1940s and came to the US where he studied at Harvard and George Washington Univ. He became the first elected president of South Korea in

1946. Rhee served until his death in 1965.

He struggled with his country's poor economy brought on by the invasion and devastation from nearly four years of war and the lack of outside support even from allies. The country had been destroyed. It would have taken a second Marshall Plan to get South Korea's industry back on its feet. He died July 19, in Honolulu HI 1965 confident he had the right decision by fighting against the invaders.

*Statue of Syngman Rhee, president of South Korea, in Seoul, Korea 1956-57*
Jack Behrens's Photo

Rhee served 3 times as president but was often criticized and called autocratic and imperialistic by members of both political parties in South Korea. During his tenure, Samsong and Hyundai would grow from pre-war businesses to large enterprises that became worldwide corporations with US help.

During our interview, I observed there were times when he would talk for a few minutes in English slowly and then would lapse into silence. I didn't know whether he was lacking oxygen or simply regrouping his thoughts. He didn't use an oxygen tank and I assumed he was not having trouble breathing but I didn't know what caused the abrupt stoppage in the discussion. I didn't see a doctor around. His wife would occasionally step in and say that he was tired and simply pausing.

The palace where we met had been opulent years earlier looking at the masonry and art work on the walls. When I was there, it was filled with dust and some debris. The building was pocked marked with shell craters from large weapons like mortar, rocket and missle rounds. It was well built, I felt, considering the kind of pounding it took from the North Korean artillery and incidental bombing by both sides.

*A shrine behind the capitol that showed no evidence of saturation bombing less than 50 yards from the nearly bombed out capitol building.*   Jack Behrens's Photo

You could tell how much had been swept up the day before by the broom marks on the floor. I mentioned it to the US liaison officer who was with us and he told me that the palace was dusted daily but that since the war, the amount of dust in the air had become overwhelming. I'm no dust expert but I kept thinking how much such air pollution was affecting all of us in that expansive hall where we met.

He never complained about a lack of support for South Korea during the war. He said that allied countries gave to the war cause and the ceasefire was the end result of very difficult fighting by troops on both sides.

His wife would continue to correct him from time to time dur-

*Gen. Mark Clark signed the ceasefire at the July 27, 1953 which didn't end the shooting but stopped artillery, mortar fire and air battles over Korea.*
U.S. Navy Museum photo

*A bombed out gun emplacement near Seoul.*
Photo by Jack Behrens

ing the interview and he didn't seem to object. His difficulties, he sighed, were a "matter of old age and the limits of the mind to answer difficult questions in a short time" with a wan smile. He pointed out that he enjoyed conversations with others in the world on topics that he felt knowledgeable about. I noticed his wife whisper to him at that point and he shook his head affirmatively.

And within about 45 minutes the interview was over. He could be crusty when he wanted to make a point. When he wanted to convey special meaning, he would return to his native tongue which was a signal for his wife to explain. Other queries he relied on her to respond in English. They worked together very well, I thought. She said that Mr. Rhee had strong feelings about what he did to try to move South Korea forward. She didn't express herself regarding her husband's opinions, I found.

He asked what I thought of the Korean people I met. I told him they impressed me as kind, very courteous and a warm people who loved farming and wanted peace so they could return to their land and crops. He smiled. His wife said that "we" (the South Koreans) are not warrior like the people from the North and we didn't like or want war but fought the best way we could. She said "South Koreans are hard working people. The people like the peace they find in their fields."

As we walked out slowly she thanked us "for coming." I felt like I had just visited a man from another century. A proud man who felt

*My momasan (foreground )waiting to do my laundry in the trickling stream not far from our Quonset just outside Seoul. Background, village huts across from the old South Korean capitol. A very shy woman who only told me her name was Lee. I think there were thousands upon thousands of Lees in Korea. I paid her one carton of Viceroys every 2 weeks*

Photo by Jack Behrens

he had done his best.

Actually, until a few years ago, I had a 50 caliber shell cartridge that I picked up when I was in the palace. That's gone now along with my Stars & Stripes ID card.

*My tiny "home" away home from for 13 months 30 miles from DMZ Korea*

Photo by Jack Behrens

Editor's Note: In a Korean War documentary, The Korean War Online said:

"Overall, the United States military was not prepared to fight the vicious infantry war that was Korea. Our political leaders had assumed the existence of nuclear weapons eliminated any effective deployment of ground forces such as was common before 1945. As a result, the quality and resolve of our fighting men varied dramatically, primarily depending on differences in their training and individual character. Still, as always, there were those special few who are always prepared. And one other fact should never be forgotten. Those whose conduct was distinguished by being awarded the Medal of Honor also represent their many comrades in arms who sacrificed themselves in obscurity."

I'd say that was an understatement. Harry Truman's decision may

*Some of my Quonset mates in Seoul left to right Manny SanGambino, UN of Maryland, left; Ralph Friedner of NYU center; Bill McCourtney of Michigan State and me (Jack) on the right*   Jack Behrens' Photo

have been right for the time... it wasn't right for a large number of Americans, some drafted or recalled to serve, who had never heard of Korea (a few who were captured said while they had gone through basic training they had no knowledge of what the conflict was about) and never realized how their government had put them at risk with poor training and obsolete weapons against very veteran Chinese and North Korean military units jacked up with their own version of moral- boosting homemade juices and narcotics. They were far tougher than American officers and soldiers thought. It was a war fought under brutal conditions in rugged mountains and urban areas of the country.

*University of Korea (once a women's college) where I taught one semester* Photo by Jack Behrens

*Organizing my trunk*  Jack Behrens' Photo

# Bob Hope

## The eternal wise cracker

He sat a row up from me in the DC-47 US Military plane. We were headed for Okinawa with stops at Guam and the Philippines. It was the annual holiday USO trip that started out on the west coast of the US and would finish back at Tachikawa Air Force Base, Tokyo.

On board for this journey of Army, Air Force, Navy bases were entertainers Bob Hope, Les Brown, Jerry Colona, the great Band of Renown, Miss Oklahoma, Dinah Shore, and about 8 beauties from Hollywood to fill the stage I think. He was wisecracking from the time we took off until we landed on Kadena runway in Okinawa.

Hope had "played" the President's Camp David one hole green in Maryland and he was talking about how Dwight Eisenhower could have orange juice without leaving his front lawn while putting at the retreat. No other president had done that, he chuckled.

Sports Illustrated carried a story that explained what happened. "There is a terrace in front of the main cabin called 'Aspen 'and then the land slopes quickly down to a small clearing that was devised by President Roosevelt. From the terrace to the edge of the wood line measured about 140 yards with about the same yardage in width. It was hardly big enough for one hole."

Golfing legend Bobby Jones designed a four hole "course" by the right edge of the green space. The first 100 yards was 15 feet above the level of the green. The second was 140 yards away and 20 feet above the green. The third was 120 yards and 20 feet below the green and the fourth was 80 yards from the green and 15 feet below the green.

Said Sports Illustrated writer Herbert Warren Wind, who wrote the piece: "It offered splendid variety of shots and no confusion in a foursome as long as each player uses a clearly distinguishable set of balls. Not sure if he might be playing with or against, Ike had his golf balls imprinted with 'MR. PRESIDENT.' The par for each hole? 3."

Hope told us the president made it easy enough for duffers but hard enough for those accomplished with the game to have to change their approach and club use. He liked to challenge others to a game of 4 hole golf.

"I figured the president had already hit so many holes in one that it was amusing for him to watch others try to hit par on his course," Bob cracked.

"Democrats don't play too many country club courses so it was a shoo-in for those who were on to the trick of low scores win. Warren Harding would have been good and Herbert Hoover probably would have too. Woodrow Wilson would still be playing in the dark," Bob laughed.

On stage at Okinawa, Hope told airmen and Marines stationed there that the Aga Khan (spiritual leader of 20 million Ismailis in Iran) had died in July and he didn't collect Social Security. "He was 79 and you can imagine what that would have done to your return on a system only 23 years old," Hope told the service personnel with a smile. The audience roared.

*Entertainer Bob Hope performs for military personnel at the USO Christmas Tour during Operation Desert Shield.*
Photo by Alamy Stock Photo

"You'll be happy to hear that the Chinese took a Great Leap Forward by putting half a billion peasants in communes where they were guaranteed food, clothing, shelter and child care," Hope said with that wry smile. "Give the friendly government agent beside you all your personal property." Again the crowd laughed for minutes.

He used some political humor and Hollywood banter for more than an hour and a half with people a long way from home. Jerry Colona did his schtick and Dinah sang "Que Sera, Sera(What Will Be, Will Be)" and tried her hand at Elvis Presley's "Love Me Tender," while Miss Oklahoma told us a little bit about her native state to catcalls from a mostly male audience. I had the pleasure of getting a kiss from her when she came stage left, had trouble with her high heels and fell into my arms. The uproar from those on that side who saw me catch her was even funnier later when Hope came back to my seat in the plane. "Well JACKAMO, good experience on Mr. Hope's pleasure boat?" I

*Bob Hope greeting our men in uniform*    US ARMY Photo

turned red and stuttered "I'm ready for another tour!"

Hope, of course, emceed the show and added those great one liners that he was best at.

"Is it true the Apaches will take the state on their way to Washington?" he asked Miss Oklahoma and she replied she wasn't aware of any uprising when she left the states. Hope quipped "They didn't know you were traveling with me did they?" The audience roared again.

The Les Brown band with stellar solos by his brother Stumpy on trombone and Dave Pell on tenor saxophone played "Leap Frog," the band's signature number, and "Autumn In New York" which caused the crowd to go silent. It was like a Christmas Carol in a desert night with the wind slowly rustling to provide a cool breeze. It didn't happen often on Okinawa I found.

Hope closed out the performance with "Thanks for the Memories" and the some 4,000 military in attendance stood and called him back for two encores.

"What do think Jackamo, good show?" he hit me on the shoulder as he passed me on his way to his seat in the front. "I loved it," I smiled. "Want to do it again?" he asked. "I'm on!" I told him. "Do you always smile like that or are those fake lips?" he joked. "They come from my mom," I said. "Don't give them back," he laughed as he sat down.

I never forgot what Bob told me during the week long tour. "Why am I so strong about doing this?" he asked no in particular. "I was born in Britain and I came to America as a kid before the war. I felt a need to give back to to my new home and those who were helping in the fight against the Nazis."

His first show for the USO was just months before the Japanese bombed Pearl Harbor, May 6, 1941. In October, 1997, members of both Houses of the US Congress passed House bill 75 which gave him honorary membership in the US Military.

*Bob Hope is given honorary membership in the US military*
Courtesy Ronald Reagan Library

"Bob Hope the status of honorary member of the US Armed Forces and the gratitude of the American people for his lifetime of accomplishments on behalf of our men and women in uniform." The first and only individual so honored in the country's history.

You earned it. Thanks, Bob for our memories and mine.

# Bill Sanders

## Award-winning cartoonist at Stars & Stripes

We only knew each other for a brief time. He was departing Korea just as I arrived. Bill Sanders, who became the new editor at STARS & STRIPES, was a great influence on those of us who believed in real stories, creative art work and no "fake" news. I never really knew what the term meant.

I had to live a long time to see journalism become trashed like law, medicine, education and other occupations of value to mankind. I remember the days when editors I worked for told us that "if you can't believe in what you read in the newspaper, what can you believe?" Of course, Mark Twain may have given us another side to consider when he said: "Get your facts first and then you can distort 'em as you please."

Bill Sanders took over and reinvigorated the Stripes and a good portion of my Korean duty. I worked as a correspondent for the US

## BILL SANDERS

military daily and sports editor of the SAC Times, an English language publication headquartered in Seoul. And I began working as an Enterprise Correspondent for the Associated Press on the civilian side.

A self-taught cartoonist, Bill was still in the military when we met. A second lieutenant from Western Kentucky University, I watched when he was a Hilltopper basketball player and I was a sports information director at Bowling Green State University (OH). He was an outstanding athlete who knew instinctively when to pass, hand off or shoot. As an SID and a person who had spent most of my life handling sports coverage, it was fun working with him. He told me he wasn't a good sports reporter, "I'd lose myself in the game I was watching," he laughed. We had a number of mutual friends from our days in the Mid-American Conference at BG and when I worked later for the Associated Press handling Big Ten Conference games at Ohio State. I knew then that writing was my life and it led to broadcast, television, newspaper, magazine and books.

Bill prepared a caricature of me that remains my logo signature today. It started with S&S and grew as I acquired an audience in a number of states

*My logo Time Out created by celebrated cartoonist Bill Sanders in Korea.*

And it earned awards for me in columns called Time Out.

I used it working for four newspapers and it continues to represent me on the web also at Time Out (www.writerjackweb.com).

I found out personally and painfully what happens when you have friends across competitive lines.

My sister Beverly's husband, Jim Hietikko, was an offensive tackle coach at Ohio State. He took a position teaching and coaching in my hometown in Lancaster. He invited me to go with him to several of Buckeye Head Coach Woody Hayes' secret skull sessions. As I learned, when it becomes family business there is hell to pay. A couple of items appeared in a neighboring paper which I had nothing to do with. It caught the attention of OSU people and Jim had to explain. He, of course, turned his anger on me. Jim was 6' 4" and about 245 pounds at the time. I was a slender 6'1" 150 pounder. I held my own verbally but I wasn't in his league physically. But I challenged him to a boxing match. He laughed so hard he nearly fell down. "I don't do such fighting," he said with another burst of laughter. We became fast friends from that day and continue today long after his unfortunate death.

Bill's philosophy for editorial cartooning was an excellent goal for those in the field today. "Make an honest attempt to stand for something or be against something in every piece of work you do," he explained to me and then later to others at a meeting of editors and writers at a conference.

"Each cartoon should be drawn for one purpose," he continued. "To convey a message. It might be flavored with humor or bitter with sledgehammer seriousness but the opinion should reach out and grab the reader by his collar. It's a tough assignment. I'm the first to admit I don't always make it either. . .but I try like hell." I always admired that honesty and work ethic.

He did it everywhere he worked. And it showed. He received his BA in English and shortly after, he married Joyce Wallace and he shipped off to Korea assigned to a mortar company as a squad leader.

At Western Kentucky, he held the NCAA's record in football for the passes completed in one season---66.8 percent---and the record continued for years. It may still be in place. He was All-Star player in both basketball and football at Pompano Beach, FL. He took a football scholarship to Western Kentucky.

He returned to Korea as a civilian with the US Army and continued on S&S before going back to the mainland. He did cartooning and sports writing in college, he told the Editor & Publisher magazine but his sports articles "were pretty awful." He worked for the English language paper Japan Times as an editorial cartoonist at night.

When he returned stateside, he was hired by the Greensboro (NC) Daily News. Bill was a part of the "New Wave" of cartoonists which challenged the status quo and jingo journalism that was obvious in the latter part of the 1950s and early 1960s. I remembered a comment passed onto me by a colleague who had heard him talk somewhere about "a vast wasteland of multi-hackneyed cartoons in the field of cartooning." I certainly agreed although a writer and photographer at the time.

*Bill Sanders, editorial cartoonist for Greensboro Daily News.*

Milton Caniff, Garry Trudeau were big names for cartoon strips not cartoons. But you can add Bill Sanders to that august list. He moved to Kansas City and worked on the Star for four years and became a nationally syndicated cartoonist. He joined the Milwaukee Journal before he retired and at the same time, moved back to his native state of Florida.

His controversies would match President Trump, Hillary or Bill Clinton for that matter. He had been at work for the Kansas City Star for a short time when the letters to the editor jumped significantly. The paper said that he had "caused more letters in a month than we've had in the last five years." The John Birch Society raised an unsuccessful drive to have Bill silenced and tried to get nearly 10,000 subscribers to drop their interest in the Star. The Saturday Review, in an article on extremists, said that the opposition had to "gag on their own breakfast."

Bill Sanders could create his own firestorm however. He sued a local Catholic Church because it disturbed the peace with its early Sunday morning bell ringing. I remember that as an Associated Press reporter in Huntington, WVA. I read the story and I heard the uproar from the opposition...even in a Bible Belt community.

Bill Sanders could zero in on hot spots in a community. I enjoyed his response to Milwaukee Mayor Henry Maier's lack of an ordinance on open housing in Milwaukee. After being called "colonel" by some for his editorial cartoons, Bill attended one of the mayor's press conferences dressed as a Kentucky Colonel and carried a chicken bucket of his sketchbook and pens. He weighed in and brought debate.

It was a pleasant surprise to me when I saw a few of his cartoons in the White House when I was there in the 1980s. Bill covered the Vietnam War as a reporter-artist prior to the Tet Offensive.

Although not an officer, I became the last editorial person standing at the Pacific Stars & Stripes. I was covering a baseball series in Seoul between the home team, EASCOM Loggers, and several divisional teams and I was looking forward to going back to Okinawa to handle a golf match between Arnold Palmer and several regional players. The temporary commanding officer when I returned to Seoul in August, 1958 was an artillery officer who knew little about newspapers, information or what to do about any of them. His advice to me: "Wait for your orders. Don't screw up. Don't get drunk. File the stories you have left to do and, for God's sake, don't put my name in any of them."

Jack (center) with two good Lancaster, OH golfers, Bill George (left) club pro and Alan Vlerebome (right) another club pro. As much as they tried to help, I still had trouble on the Camp David 4 hole. I played it when I visited the camp. I hit par.
Jack Behrens' Photo

I later covered Palmer and Jack Nicklaus exhibition matches near Jack's home in Upper Arlington, OH shortly after I returned and joined the Lancaster paper. The S & S Korea Bureau closed about a month after I finally left. War time brings strange coincidences and even stranger relationships.

POSTSCRIPT: The Army offered me several "surprise" gifts on the way out. Each of us who boarded the aging, old troop ship USS Breckenridge for the 21 day trip (made longer because the US Defense Department had miscalculated the troop levels throughout the world.) I served as editor of the Breckenridge News ship newspaper. First, we were required to take 20 knee-high stockings each in our individual duffel bags to turn in port side in Fort Lewis, Seattle, WA. (if we didn't have them we had to pay the military $35 per pair)! The second gift was the loss of leave time when we returned because of the delay. The delay, incidentally, was because troop levels were down and the Army decided to keep us on duty during our departure trip. The $350 my first wife Patty and I were counting on to start our life again was taken from my pay. I used up two weeks just getting back to Ohio. I received $200 instead of $400. Thank you for your service.

# Duke Ellington

## Interviewing Duke Ellington

I met Duke Ellington at a dance he played at the Crystal Ballroom at Buckeye Lake, OH. Duke was as dapper as ever and he had that quick smile as his eyes danced around the empty dance floor. He was plinkiing on the sturdy upright piano and listening intently for the sound several keys made in an open air dance pavilion. He shook his head.

"Acoustics aren't the best," he said. "But with the saxophones and trumpets and the rhythm section it will get people on the dance floor. We like to play for couples dancing. That's what America likes, dancing."

You had to love the man who could coast into a slow number like Sophisticated Lady and swing on to a great arrangement of Satin Doll with grace and ease. It came naturally to Edward Kennedy Ellington.

I was with my future first wife, Patty, my date that Friday. I picked her up at 4 pm. "Why so early for a dance that starts at 9?" she asked. I told her I thought I could meet some of the guys in the band. She looked at me with her very big beautiful eyes and rolled them. That was always a sign she thought I was on another one of my "dream clouds" she called them.

"Isn't it an all-Black orchestra? Who do you know? I thought you said that you didn't have more than one Black family in Lancaster?" she asked innocently. I ignored her question and told her that this was a band powered by the great Jo Jones on drums and some terrific side men. "I'm impressed," she said sarcastically with a response that said she wasn't. "Wait until you hear them," I encouraged.

Later, after we had squeezed on the crowded dance floor she told me she agreed. We danced more than we had ever done to beautiful 2/4 tempos and even tried our hand at some Latin numbers. "I've never tried to dance to such music," she said quietly and out of breath when we went back to the table. Duke was in good form that night. He introduced some of the members of the band and I told Patty what I knew about them. There was Johnny Hodges, alto sax; and Lawrence Brown on trombone and the great Cootie Williams on trumpet and she interrupted "I'm totally impressed that you think they're great," she added and said "let's walk."

As we walked and took in the lake breeze off the water, I told her about Duke's background and what he wrote. "He also wrote church music too," I said. That aroused her curiosity. Patty was an organist in a small Fairfield County (OH) village and enjoyed playing hymns on a church pipe organ.

Duke's parents raised him in a middle class neighborhood of the nation's capitol and insisted that he "mind his manners" he told me that night with a smile. "My parents were musicians and they knew the value of being courteous and to have respect for white and black folks of all ages," Duke continued. They did well in America at a time when the races were separated. "You knew instinctively what you could do and what wasn't acceptable." It was a learning experience. "I watched and gained from what I saw," he added.

He had assembled a 12 piece orchestra by 1930 and recorded such numbers as his own compositions Black and Tan Fantasy and the Mooche. At 41, he was leading a group of talented Black musicians such as Hodges, Sam Nanton, Williams, Jones and later, a talented white drummer named Louie Bellson, who used a double bass drum set.

The Ellington Orchestra was on the road all over the country to play dances, concerts and even in churches. Always very sophisticated and elegantly dressed, Duke called it his "orchestra" not band as he toured. He logged about 20,000 performances in the US and 65 countries throughout the world.

His signature tune "Take the A Train" came from a gifted Black composer –piano player Billy Strayhorn who joined him for a time. Ellington was helped along by the advancement of radio and a Black nightclub called "The Cotton Club" in the Harlem section of New York City where he drew white and black crowds for a number of years.

At the Crystal ballroom that warm night, we made our way through a throng of people to our table and met a Black couple who had come while we were out and asked politely to join us because they couldn't find seats. The couple was from nearby Columbus and they knew Duke better than I did. It was a great evening. Patty became an Ellington fan for the moment and we danced several more times before we decided we should leave. The couple said we should "stay in touch."

Duke, of course, was destined for greatness. He received honorary degrees including the distinguished Presidential Medal of Freedom from President Lyndon Johnson and France gave him the Legion of Honor, the highest honors the two countries could offer such talent.

It all happened on my watch. It was the beginning of what I thought would be a future playing drums. It came to an end one day after I returned from service while we were living in a walk up apartment in Lancaster.

We didn't have space for a large array of drums, hi-hat cymbal stand and other pieces that I used. I didn't argue and she didn't press me to do it. But it was a decision I knew I had to make. I sold my Slingerland set to a photographer friend Biff Barr. Ironically, it was the set used by Kenny Carpenter, Bandleader Dick Trimble's drummer, the man I replaced.

I didn't know until later my father had contacted him to find a set. Kenny said he was leaving the business and told dad he'd give him a deal. My mom had hounded my father for weeks to get a set. In making the deal, my dad sold Kenny an insurance policy on his car. The Art of the Deal alive before President Trump was 1 year old.

It all happened four days before I started with Trimble and owned a home made set of snare drum, battered hi-hat sock cymbal contraption and sticks.

Before Patty and I left the ballroom that night we danced toward Duke and said good night. Duke gave us his typical comment to fans: "I love you madly."

# WALT DISNEY

## A Giant Among Geniuses

Can you imagine what Walt Disney would say if he saw what is happening on TV and in film today? I can. He probably would express dismay for the lack of creativity I see but admiration for the technical advances.

I met Walt by accident on a Northwest Orient Stratoliner (I think that's what it was called in the late 1950s) headed for Chicago from Columbus, OH. He had been visiting family in Ohio and was headed for Los Angeles.

I was going to a job interview with Elks Magazine in Chicago. I was an applicant for one of the number of part-time positions I took in the 1960s into the 1990s. I recognized him when I sat down beside him on the comfortable seat. His mustache was the give away. Much like my father's I thought.

"Mr. Disney, it's a pleasure to be making the trip with you," I started.

"Please, he interrupted, the only Mr. in Disney Studios is Mr. Lessing, our lawyer," he responded. "Walt is fine."

I apologized for the slight and then trying to show him I knew something about his work in films I said I enjoyed 'Peter Pan'.
"I didn't," he curtly replied.

Pause. When you're trying to start a conversation the one thing you don't want to do is irritate the subject before you start. I was off to a disastrous landing before takeoff I thought!

"Was there a problem in production?" I asked.

He smiled and said "No, the characters lacked warmth and heart. Simply missed what we intended to give our audience," he replied. "Did you see Bambi?" he said with a smile. "Yes, I did. And I loved it. It certainly displayed heart and much warmth," I replied with the hope that I had mentioned something HE did like. "Ánd I enjoyed Dumbo which I saw a year earlier," I added.

"Well Disney Studios is very happy you are a fan," he retorted with a chuckle. "I'm happy to be a very inquisitive guy and when I see things I don't like or think are right, I start thinking things don't have to be like this. I think it's kind of fun to do the impossible."

I asked him how you assemble such talent and make films so family centered and pleasing. It wasn't my world certainly as a hard news and sports editor who never gave much thought to fantasy in a world that was trying to forget World War II and trying to ignore what was happening in Indo-China. "I tell everyone that our people are the very best at what they do. And they feel open to contribute to each production by suggestions and make us feel we're provided something unique. That makes my job easier and satisfying," he said with an ease that drew my attention.

I had interviewed many people overseas and in the US and here was clearly a man who loved his workforce. "I have very excellent artists and animators as well as technicians who excite me with what they do every day," he beamed. I've said a number of times and I believe it to be true: I don't make pictures just to make money. I make money to make more pictures. I'm not interested in pleasing the critics. I'll take my chances pleasing the audiences."

*Walt Disney 1954*     Wikipedia / NASA

"What do you do?" he asked with curiosity. "I just finished a tour of duty in Korea working as a sports writer-editor and a stint with Pacific Stars & Stripes newspaper as a correspondent," I responded.

"Exciting?" he inquired. "I was a draftee who never expected to get to do what I did in the military. I gained a lot of experience and saw more than I ever want to see of what war can do to a country," I answered.

"How do you write about sports in a war zone?" he asked somewhat amused.

"The military does a much better job than people think at trying to give troops something from home. Each base and division and air squadrons have baseball, football and basketball teams and travel to other locations to play games. There are some good college athletes here who want to keep playing and the military has made it possible with all kinds of support," I explained.

He then told me about his experience with the Red Cross when he and Ray Kroc, later founder and CEO of McDonalds, trained as ambulance drivers in World War I. He never finished high school, he told me. He dropped out of school to join the army. "That was supposed to be the war that would end all wars. It wasn't sadly and look at how it got worse when everybody thought it would get better," he said with shrug.

I said that my father has a mustache somewhat like his and he smiled and said that "some at Disney think that I'm unfair because I don't let other males on the staff have them. I use it as an image for who I represent and who I am. To have others represent us especially to children I feel is wrong. It represented the wrong kind of image," he answered softly.

I was perspiring as I continued to pull every lever in my brain to recall all I could about Walt. I had no notes to review, no real knowledge other than the films I saw and some clips about him I had read sometime back before my service days. Interviews come sometimes at a moment's notice. You have to be prepared!

He asked out of the blue if I liked model trains. "Yes, I do, in fact, I've got a classic Lionel 12 car freight with box cars and a caboose. I've had it since I was about 11 or 12. My parents got it for me for Christmas and I set it up in the basement. It came down when my first wife, Patty, and I moved into our walk-up apartment. Couldn't put the train set and my drums in the bedroom and open the bathroom door!"

"I hope you don't get rid of the train set," he said with a quick smile. "You"ll enjoy it again someday." I was busy searching for more paper to take notes . . .and he was gone.

He was anxious to get off the plane to get something to eat, he said. "I need a hamburger and I hope to find a piece of lemon merinque pie or chocolate ice cream soda," he said as we both prepared to leave.

"It's been a pleasure," I said. "No the pleasure was mine," he smiled and then said "have a good life. And don't forget to keep that train set."

"By the way," he said looking back at me, "you'll have to come to Holmby Hills, CA to see mine. It's life-sized and surrounds my house."

I kept my drums, Walt.

Jack Behrens' Photo

# Tom Clancy

## An imaginative military writer

He was funny, opinionated, argumentive and yet he was very believable. Incredible as it was...he was talking about a Russian sub that surfaced off the US coast. Not uncommon today. It was in the 1950s and '60s.

That's how the author of *The Hunt For Red October*, Tom Clancy, described how he put together his best selling novel to my magazine writing class a number of years ago. He showed up with dark glasses and sneakers. He caught everybody's attention. Even several students in the backrow with their eyes closed.

With tensions mounting in the world every hour, people are more alert today...for their own safety if nothing else. Yet, a good part of the country, regardless of political party, have little idea of what is happening. It reminds me of what it must have been like in the beginning when Britain was enforcing it's rule of law on America here in the colonies.

Clancy told me that he was never really a part of the press nor was he a member of the "writing field.' People continued to label me a 'correspondent' 'journalist' 'writer' and other titles but I don't think I fit any of those," he grinned.

Like so many who don't understand the writing world, we both had the dilemma of defending our seemingly sloppy habits of keeping slips of paper and torn corners of newspapers and magazines all over our desks which frequently would end up on the floor along with bits of pieces of scribbled notes. We smiled at each other when we were asked why writers are so cluttered in their personal habits.

"You can't defend it," he chuckled as he responded to an inquiry from the audience. "My wife was in the insurance business and she said it came from poor study habits as a kid. I was in the business too and I thought it was an over-active brain that couldn't keep track of all the information. Whatever it was, I found a good number of writers suffered the same affliction. I never worried about it. But it did seem to worry others more."

How can writers get things right in such confusion? "I think because we edit, tighten and rewrite so much. It's a combination of discipline and habit that drives you to finish," he said.

Tom Clancy died 2013 but before he did, he left us with a number of exciting tales that pitted the Soviet Union against United States. Where did a former Maryland insurance broker get such information? How was he able to get on the national stage?

"Going to cocktail parties and embassy receptions and just listening to idle chatter," he answered. "You would be amazed how talkative people are with a drink or two as they try to be exciting to an unknown guest or two," he said with a smile. "I was startled at times by how much they offered in just normal conversation."

But how credible were those he talked to? "They were generals with stars on their shoulders or admirals with chevrons up their sleeves." Tom was discussing how he collected his data and created his novel and others that followed.

"My books didn't come from thin air," he told the class. "They

*On Art Levy's afternoon show on WKTV NBC, Utica, NY*   Jack Behrens' Photo

came from real people in responsible high positions," he continued. They make decisions that can cause death or keep people alive. It used to sound like a true fiction thriller until we started seeing such stories take place. Read the papers, listen to news accounts or watch TV news! Novelists certainly let things get loose. But there is a need to keep stories realistic and credible for discerning readers. Tom did just that.

Novelists are obviously attentive readers and alert to details. They liked others who share their interest in books. He believed President Ronald Reagan had much to do with the success of his first book. In

2002, he told an interviewer "President Reagan, was actually a big reader, and he read the book during his tenure at the White House, and liked it and he talked it up and Time magazine found out and. . . did an article about it and I became a bestselling author."

Hardly as simple as that but Clancy was hardly a typical novelist. Said reviewer John Sutherland in the Guardian, "Tom Clancy is not, by conventional literary criteria, a great novelist. But he, without question, (is) the novelist with the biggest ideological clout currently active."

*Clancy at Boston College*
Photo by Gary Wayne Gilbert / Wikipedia

In class that day he told students that to claim to be a writer is a bigger challenge than most people and even writers understand. "There is no such thing as writer's block. Writer's block is the official term for being lazy. You don't get royalty checks from being lazy in this work."

Clancy had no military or espionage experience. He didn't serve in the armed services. Nor did he set out to be a writer either. He was an avid reader of everything pertaining to the military. He did, however, find ways to get himself invited to many parties and outings where he was rubbing shoulders with military people. He learned to "talk the talk" and become an authority on military hardware and tactics. One military officer I talked to who was among naval brass at a party told me he watched Clancy carefully discuss strategy with colonels and navy ensigns who had been in wars and staff meetings and he "held his own and managed to take the lead in chats."

Tom was invited to speak to military audiences and had a good number of friends in various branches of the US security and the Defense Department. He had a keen awareness of current events. Back in the days when Osama Bin Laden was alive and on the prowl, Clancy told me: "He never sent me any fan mail and I haven't really sold many books in Afghanistan but I realized that he was a serious threat to our nation." Of his research he said: "I read the papers, watch CNN and think. It's in the open…you just have to know where to look."

He also let people in his neighborhood and elsewhere know what he did, too. He had an M4A1 army tank on his front lawn and a shooting range in his basement.

He was the author of 17 New York Times bestsellers including *The Hunt For Red October, Clear and Present Danger, The Sum of All Fears* and *Patriot Games,* created the military character CIA agent Jack Ryan who was, said Clancy, "an improved version of himself without the need for an ophthalmologist to get his eyes fixed" and introduced branding (placing a logo or identifying signature on the item or car) of his creations that earned him $35 million by 2007-08. It all started with the first novel *The Hunt for Red October* which first sold for a mere $5,000 to the small publishing house, Naval Institute Press.

In 1996, Clancy returned President Reagan's glowing comments by dedicating his book Executive Orders to "Ronald Wilson Reagan, 40th president of the United States: the man who won the war."

# John Slade

## Teacher, Philosopher, Author

Good friend John Slade once lived in the beautiful Adirondacks in upstate New York. A graduate of Cornell University, Ithaca, NY, John spent his summers camping and hiking in the wilderness of the Empire state but he became disillusioned with young people he taught at several colleges. John taught English as a second language and other topics. I found him to be a very broadly educated man of opinions and not afraid to share his thoughts … or accept others' thoughts.

He was a frequent guest on my CBS-WIBX regional radio show while I taught at Utica College, NY over the course of 10 years, an outdoorsman, a naturalist and a writer now with a number of books on Amazon and Barnes & Noble. John's unhappiness finally caused him to move to Oslo, Norway, to teach after spending a number of years teaching Russian students English.

He especially enjoyed UC college engineer, Bill Parker, who was the son of a minister and sparked more arguments than I could handle in the 30 minute tapes we did. A quiet, unassuming man of knowledge and without a degree, Bill was a consummate reader who frequently made me wonder whether I hosted the program ... or he did. But we worked well together. I still miss his sardonic sense of humor.

*John Slade at home in Oslo, Norway*
Jack Behrens' Photo

Here's how John explained his reasons for leaving his native America.

"I taught in St. Petersburg and Arkhangelsk during the 1990s. It was the decade of the severe depression in Russia. I was teaching at a graduate school in northern Norway and in 1991, we received funding from the Norwegian government to start an exchange program with one or more universities in Russia. I visited Russian classrooms from October 1991, right through the decade, usually for one or two week visits when I could fit it with my teaching in Norway."

He took a sabbatical from graduate school in Saint Petersburg, Russia. "I liked my Russian students so much that I wanted to live and teach full time at Baltic State Technical University in Saint Petersburg. Conditions at that time were comparable to conditions in America during the worst of our Depression. The university during that winter was never warmer than 45 degrees. We had frost on the classroom windows and my students wore their coats and scarves and boots all day in classes. My own tiny apartment was just as cold. I slept in a Norwegian down sleeping bag."

What really impressed him was his students. "Jack, my Russian students were the best I have ever taught during my entire career. They were highly motivated, far beyond American and Norwegian students. They were friendly, respectful, always helpful. If I assigned on a Monday a three-page essay on Friday, they turned in five to ten pages on Friday, written and rewritten and in their absolute best English."

Classroom discussions were terrific; we discussed life in Russia and they all would contribute with vehement opinions, he told me. Their general attitude in Saint Petersburg was very positive. Their view toward Europe was also positive. Gorbachev had opened the borders and Russians could travel if they had the money. It was 1989.

"Russians felt they could reach out to the West in genuine friendship," John said. The Russians let the small republics such as Latvia, Lithuania and Estonia become independent. They pulled their troops from Poland and "reached out to the West with genuine friendship." They requested that NATO not put their troops near Russia's border.

"Personally, I often saw Russians in Saint Petersburg wearing clothing with the American flag on the back of a shirt. They carried shopping bags with the American flag on both sides of the bag. The kids especially wore T-shirts and sweatshirts with American logos. I never felt threatened as an American. People were always friendly, always welcoming."

America didn't respond with friendship.

Europe, however, did. "European Countries continued setting

up mutual educational programs such as the one I participated in Norway. Swedish banks invited Russian bank workers to attend a month of classes during the summer. The Russians stayed at Swedish colleges and attended classes in English. "The Russians loved their time in Sweden learning English and their new experiences and banks began learning how to work together more efficiently," John noted.

"I saw few signs of American educational cooperation in Russia," he continued. "What I did see, abundantly, were HUGE billboards all over St. Petersburg advertising Marlboro and Camel cigarettes and Coca-Cola. These companies were trying, as Russians would tell you, to put Russian cigarettes and soft drinks out of business. The Russians, including my students, began to tell me how their attitudes were changing."

"Americans," they said, "always want Russia to appear weak. Americans want to be superior and put us down," Russian students told John.

When he returned to America in 1995 to take care of his parents (who live in Stuart, FL) he wrote a new book 'about my experiences in Russia,' he told me. It's called The New Saint Petersburg: 1991-1996.

"I discovered that Americans, including my family and friends, were not in the slightest bit interested in Russia and with the help of high oil prices, Putin (Russian president) managed a steady increase in prosperity," John wrote me. "The same old attitude ---you can't trust the Russians, the Russians are our enemy---prevailed in America. He (Putin) managed a steady increase in prosperity."

The Russians, I felt, admire Putin because he brought order to Russia and because they believe he is a strong leader who stands up to the Americans.

"The Americans always crush Russia's dignity whereas Putin

gave them their dignity back. Yes, the Russians marched into Ukraine but, as they will tell you, they did far less damage than America did in 2003, when we blasted our way into Iraq. Now, both countries are deeply involved in the war in Syria and NATO forces and equipment are pressing against the Russian borders in several European countries. We are right back to the Bad Old Days," John continued.

"We had a historic opportunity to build a genuine friendship with Russia. We squandered that opportunity," he concluded.

Obviously, a number agree and a number disagree. This country is in that type of disarray in 2017.

When will we reread our own history books? When will we admit to our mistakes? And, when will all of us in this cancerous political environment admit our errors in judgment?

God told us to "forgive those who transgress against us." Forgiving others is unfortunately not in our "wheel house." Too much pride, I think. But I admit to be ordinary and very human.

John Slade offers us a different view but one he has lived.

# James Michener

## A Meticulous Best-Selling Author

I was in dusty summer military fatigues. James Michener was dressed appropriately for the temperature (near 90) and dry weather.. "Do you mind if I sit here too?" He asked nonchalantly. I told him I was visiting but shaken after a landing at Kadena (airport). I started to explain and he interrupted by telling me "you'll get use to that ," he said abruptly as a huge road grading machine started with a roar and rumbled by us.

We sat for another 15 minutes as the road grader moved past.
"Where are you from?" I said trying to make polite conversation.
"Doylestown, Bucks County," he replied..

"That's in Pennsylvania," I replied. "Correct," he said somewhat irritated by my lack of geography.

"I assume you're military," he inquired. "Yes, sir," I said.

"I'm not an officer actually I'm a visitor too. I'm a writer doing research on a book I'm writing on a beautiful island, Hawaii," he added.

My mind was searching my memory for a writer from Doylestown, PA. "I'm James Michener, he said and you are?"

"I'm PFC Jack Behrens with Stars & Stripes," I stammered.

Well, PFC Jack, do you write, take photos or sell the paper?" he added with a slight grin. "No sir, I'm a writer too," I responded.

"And what do you write?" he questioned. "Reviews, features, USO shows and sports," I said. "Do you enjoy it?" he asked. "Sure," I responded.

We talked about writing and writers and he told me that "far too few writers edit themselves critically. It's one of the reasons that there's little literature that rises to quality today (1950s). I believe it's symptomatic of education that doesn't stress the need for editing. Most teachers return papers to students with more questions than answers about what was submitted. I realize as every teacher does ---I taught too---that you have to spend a considerable amount of time to carefully examine a manuscript today. It's more than just punctuation and spelling. It's context and syntax and meaning of words. But that has to be done to be complete," he told me.

But what about the teachers' complaint that they simply don't have the time? I asked.

"True," he said but that doesn't eliminate the problem does it?"

We both agreed it doesn't. "The most important question is finding a way to improve the quality of what is put on paper not increase the quantity. It's as simple as that yet it doesn't completely answer the problem either."

I then remembered he wrote the movie story The Bridges of Toko-ri a great action/love story of the Korean war (I saw it twice).

"I was on this island shortly before I went aboard the aircraft carrier group," Michener told me. "I asked permission to meet with air crews. It was given. Their stories formed the backdrop for the movie. It fit the time and the emotions of the country," Michener noted. The film starred William Holden, Grace Kelly, Frederic March and Mickey Rooney.

An all-star cast and it had an impact on the American public. The raid was planned by Navy Commander Paul N. Gray and it was carried out with rules of engagement which were placed on pilots not to drop their payloads on bridges that crossed the Yalu River in North Korea. Two squadrons of McDonnell Banshee and Douglas Skyraider jets and a number of prop planes carried out the raid from carriers about 100 miles off the east coast of Korea during the brutally cold winter of 1951-52. The American public became very aware of the cost of war when it was announced that 30 percent of the airmen involved were shot down.

For the first time pilots were going off to war aboard carriers and coming home for supper or turning up missing or dead in mangled aircraft somewhere in the ocean. A good number were reservists from WWII. It showed us how what we thought we fought for didn't end.

## JAMES MICHENER

"I was active in the Buck County Democratic Party and I decided to run for Congress." Although his wife told him it wasn't a good idea, he ran. "She kept saying don't do it. I felt I should. I lost." he shrugged. "I went back to what I did best, writing books," he smiled.

at 8th Army and while flying one of two missions over the DMZ in North Korea...Because of an old Army map dated 1945, We flew about 50 miles into North Korea. We discovered Pageour error when I heard the pings of rifle and saw bullets hit our fuselage.   Jack Behrens' Photo

He talked about writing for television. It didn't work. "Too restrictive for me," he told me as he picked up a clump of sand. "Producing a show in an hour is not a writer's problem but it becomes that when you consider how to break to fit advertising and station breaks and other distractions. See how fast the sand slips through my hand? That's how the story line can be lost on the screen and it makes the writer work harder to deliver and create interest," he told me. He mentioned that he did work with a television series called "Adventures in Paradise" which he felt came closer to what he felt could be done. (1959)

For years, James Michener was the most popular writer in the United States. Tom Clancy and Danielle Steel are close but his lifetime total of 75 million novels sold still holds. His blockbusting documentary Centennial became a 12 part miniseries on NBC from October, 1978 to January, 1979. It was taken from his massive detailed study of several generations of families in the American West.

As a writer, his lifetime production is not only impressive it's awesome. According to the State House Press, which published a Michener bibliography from 1923 to 1995, there were 2,500 titles. I believe there are more to be added.

In fact, Michener told me that he spent 12 to 15 hours per day at his large desk electric typewriter for 72 years and his filing system couldn't keep up with his production. By comparison, I spent more than 60 years writing and publishing approximately 10,000 articles and columns, 24 books, textbooks and commentary. He started writing when he was 40 while a Naval historian in the Pacific. He was a lieutenant in the Navy. His notes and impressions became the Tales of the South Pacific (1947). The adaptation became a Rodgers and Hammerstein Broadway musical that won a Pulitzer for fiction in 1948.

We talked about production and he said that, like Danielle Steel, he tried to put family at the top of his daily agenda. "But it didn't always happen."

His married life showed the difficulty of work and leisure and the dilemma of balance. His first marriage to Patti Koon came to an end 13 years later. The same year, 1948, he married Vange Nord.

He met his third wife, Mari Yoriko Sabusawa at a Chicago luncheon. An American, Mari and her Japanese parents had been interned during World War II. His novel Sayonara, was considered quasi-autobiographical. Set in the early 1950s, it told the story of an American Air Force pilot stationed in Japan who fell in love with a Japanese woman describing how the two continued their relationship in a country occupied by American servicemen and women including their cross-cultural romance during a period of racism in the post-war era. It was adapted into a highly successful movie starring Marlin Brando, James Garner, Miko Taka and Red Buttons. Buttons won the Academy Award for best supporting actor.

James Michener, an orphan adopted by a Quaker woman, Mabel Michener, became a major donor to a number of educational, cultural and writing institutions including his alma mater, Swathmore College, where he received his bachelor's degree in English and history summa cum laude.

His first job was teaching English at George School, Newtown, PA from 1933 to 1936 and then he attended Colorado State College of Education (renamed University of Northern Colorado) where he received a Master of Arts degree. Several years after his first marriage he became a guest lecturer at Harvard. He joined MacMillan Publishers as it's Social Studies editor at the end of his first year at Harvard.

He was one of the first established writers to contribute to the Iowa Writers Workshop, I remember. He also gave more than $37 million to the University of Texas at Austin. His gifts to the University at Austin made him the single largest donor at the time. His philanthropy was obvious and generous.

Years after his death, Steve Berry edited a final booklet, a 126 page pamphlet called Presidential Lottery. He felt strongly about the Electoral System; he believed it was a disaster and should be replaced. He offered his suggestions, too. His comments should be required reading for every new congressman or woman I think.

Suffering from terminal kidney disease he died at 90. He had beautiful memories of the New Hebrides (now Vanuatu) in the Pacific, he said in his final years.

"During the Pacific War years," he wrote, "I served in those beautiful islands. While those beautiful islands have changed much with progress in the ensuing years, I know from subsequent visits that the friendliness of the peoples, the infectious smiles and their open-heartedness will remain forever one of life's treasures."

The informal interview, although short, was one of my best and impressed me with the motivation to become a writer.

# JESSICA MITFORD

## Dying in America is Expensive

I interviewed Jessica at Utica College's MacFarlane Auditorium when she was 49 after she lectured a group about the American Way of Death. It was 1968 and death and dying were popular subjects as the war in Vietnam continued.

Her own death in July, 1996, was hardly noticed some said. But her work on death and how to accept it lives on.

She believed Americans had been sold on a lavish way to die. With her very strong British accent she told students with a wry smile "Gracious dying in this country(US) is a macabre and an expensive joke on the American public."

Her book took American readers by storm. The cost of putting a body in the ground was approaching $6500 at the time and there was little interest in cremation, a cheaper way to pass on without taking from family finances. Today, the cost of an inground funeral with all the "trappings" a word she used to describe all the extras, can be $15,000 or more.

"The Greatest Generation" in America brought the increase in spiraling cost of death it appears. If you go to cemeteries around the US you will find a reminder of how much was spent on gravestones and monuments in the United States. Graves from the 1800s to 1950s are strikingly different than those from earlier decades. They were larger and required much more stone-cutting and chiseling to complete.

My grandfather, who bought a plot for my grandmother and himself, decided to have a large monument put in place that was bigger than stones close by. It took months for the work to be done. It cost plenty but it was what my grandad wanted. He was satisfied and the family was happy.

The flower market got a boost by yearly increases in deaths, too. Jessica told those assembled at the college that day in the rebellious '60s that "you can't just buy a simple spray. That says you are merely acknowledging the death. You have to buy lavish displays that show your real feelings. The number of flowers and the cost are important. Add to that the florist you choose and how they prepare the arrangement." Amused by her own description she added "it was an American phenomenon like Barnum & Bailey Circuses. The showing of the body, the casket, the procession to the church or to the cemetery, the hours of respectful mourning and the reading of the will. Just a bit much I feel."

As a photographer who used to take photos as a side business, I remember a few funerals that are still unforgettable. Grostesque really. One family called me when I wrote obituaries in my hometown in Lancaster, OH and asked if I would come to a funeral home and take photos of the family. When I got there, an uncle of the deceased came to me and told me he wanted photos of the dead relative with him.

"That may mean propping up the body and I don't know whether that can be done," I told him as politely as I could. "I want every member of the family to have individual photos with a beloved uncle," he said firmly. If the funeral home director agrees I'll try, I said.

It took three hours of shooting twelve people, one by one, standing, kneeling, sitting and bending over to kiss the deceased. I did it. I was paid $450 for my time and the 8 ½ X 11 black and white prints. He was satisfied but I was uneasy about what I had done. And I told myself there has to be a better way to make part-time income.

In 1939, the Mitfords-- Jessica and Esmond-- emigrated to the US from England. Esmond died in 1941. She married again in 1943 and she and her new husband Robert Treuhaft lived in America and traveled.

As a writer she gained an image much like John Dos Passo and Sinclair Lewis. Their messages cut across the grain. So did hers. It may have cut into the fabric of the funeral industry. It didn't eliminate flowers from funerals but it caused people to review the value along with the price of an obituary. "It can cost a family hundreds of dollars if they try to let people in different states know about the death of a father who was born in a city in Iowa after he moved to Florida," a funeral director told me.

A photographer added "we still do funerals but nothing very elaborate or more than for the immediate family."

Jessica says that what she discovered in her research was that Americans are so traumatized by death that they frequently don't take any steps to deal what must be done until it's virtually too late. They are too frequently caught in grief and can't get past their feelings at a time when important decisions have to be made. Sometimes, within hours.

Emotions still are the crucial element and grief plays heavy into guilt to do more to show your feelings, I discovered. "Some who are prominent in the community take on the burden of making sure that the family name gets the importance it needs especially if survivors want to keep the name alive and respected. That's always the case where there's a business that must protect the future," an editor friend told me at the elaborate funeral of a business owner who was suspected of dying of a drug overdose. The obituary tells the story but few publications want to end a lucrative relationship with a truthful story of death that ends business as usual.

Her book, which exposed some of the sales gimmicks that funeral homes use to sell expensive funerals was a hit in both England and US because it hit a nerve. From flowers to caskets and services, the funeral industry has been offering more services and the add ons have continued to increase the cost of dying.

Added to that is the space issue. Many cemeteries are running out of land and inground plots therefore raising the costs of embalming a body and burying it. Veterans have discovered that even the national cemetery in Arlington, DC. has limits.

Jessica wrote about it in a humorous way which created more interest because the subject for so long was something not discussed even among family members. "Go home and tell your parents to save their money. Don't spend it all putting mum and dad to rest," she ended. Applause showed she hit a nerve.

# AL NEUHARTH

### The man who built Gannett newspapers

Al became a longtime friend when I met him at a Newspaper Association convention in Chicago. We spent time on the phone, at several newspaper editors' conferences and he accepted my invitations to speak to my journalism classes at Utica College in New York.

UC had gained prominence for its coupling of liberal arts and professional programs, a mixture on a college campus I had never seen before. Public relations, thanks to a spry, dynamic man, Raymond Simon, became a fast rising specialty in career education at UC.

Far too many politicians, ex-newsmen and women as well as bureaucrats who drifted in and out of government, education and an assortment of corporations got into newpaper work without real credentials because they were hired by friends of the publisher or staff members.

## AL NEUHARTH

They could write, in some cases, but they had no idea of what PR meant. Or newspaper work, for that matter. They believed they had a license to say what they wanted to without thinking about the consequences of their words or context. It's still a problem.

There were far too many opinionmakers, far to little actual reporting, he told a conference for editors I attended. It got worse during the Vietnam War and later. Television added to the din.

One look at today's media shows we haven't solved the issue either.

Al was a hard-charging publisher who spoke plain facts to many editorial people who didn't always understand the facts of the business of print journalism in the late '60s and '70s. Even into the '80s. Several editors I knew, for example, called me when he took over managing Gannett after Paul Miller, then chairman of the board, stepped back and let Al manage the operation from its headquarters in Rochester, NY.

Neuharth was a South Dakotan who had graduated from the University of South Dakota after WWII. He had joined the US Army at 19 and served with the 86th Infantry in France and Germany and, later in the Philippines.

I joined the UC faculty not yet tenured back from service, after

*Here I am (left) with two good friends, Dick Westbrook, news director and Dick Schorr, sports director both of WHOK from reporting days in Ohio covering Lancaster sports. We had to keep our own statistics.*   Photo by Biff Barr

leaving Pacific Stars & Stripes, Seoul, Korea-Tokyo, Japan, when my Army service was completed. I returned to the states to take a sports editor's position in my hometown of Lancaster, OH.

A few years later, after I left Lancaster, Al bought the paper added it to the Utica, NY daily and more than 70 others in North America, including the St. Luce News Tribune, FL.

I had been with the Stars & Stripes as a correspondent and been asked to stay. If I stayed, the military would have shipped my household goods and car---even our cat---to Tokyo and the salary was close to what I would have received on a stateside paper.

Had I left before the required three –year-stint was up, I'd have had to pay my way back to the states along with my household, wife and our cat. I really wanted my wife to have input. She thought that we both would miss our families given the distance and the cost of trying to return on vacations.

I put that question to Al when I met him in the late 1960s. in Utica.

"Bad decision," he said.

"What can you do in Utica or Lancaster that would be comparable to what you could do on Stripes?" he asked. "Look at the bigger picture," he retorted. I didn't take his advice but I appreciated his honesty.

*Taking a break with my constant companion at 57 Stebbins Dr, Clinton, NY, Cleo. She liked my company but vanished when I had to take her to the vet for shots.* Jack Behrens' Photo

I satisfied my first wife Patty and our cat (Cleo the cat had no interest in travel period) but I was always wondering as many people do about leaving one place to go elsewhere.

"As a bread winner looking to the future, large image organizations are better for growth than places where you standstill and risk falling back," he replied. I never forgot his advice. But I chose family.

For several years, Al made visits to my reporting, editing and media law classes once or twice each semester. If he couldn't connect, we set up telephone conference calls. We enjoyed each other and he was interested in student reaction to the newspaper business and, of course, Gannett.

He sat in on my reporting and editing courses and we visited the UC library. He gave the college $250,000 for further development.

He was excited about the way I was able to persuade a liberal arts faculty to accept the fact that I needed more courses in what I called "field work in Journalism." It was actual work for so many hours a week for area newspapers and radio stations after two years of basic theory and practical work in the field. Faculty in those days liked theory over practice and they were doubtful of the outcome. In fact, they were very negative.

There was even reluctance from some editors and broadcasters about putting students on actual assignments. Unions weren't happy and some staff members even told me that it wasn't "their job to recruit or teach." I told Al and he said "I'll send them a note ---or their publishers---to back your plan. It's the only way we're going to get students into what the work really is. This isn't brain surgery, it's asking good questions after doing solid research and then writing factual stories you can defend. It's solid practicum." To have editors and broadcasters who were experienced assisting young people who could becoming beginning reporters was a good start.

I had successes and some failures. So did Al. In his first venture with fellow South Dakota graduate Bill Porter, they called SoDak

Sports, the publication went bankrupt within a year.

I wrote myself a note about the first two years after I had placed 20 students on five area news departments. The amount of hypocrisy I found among editors and reporters who were to evaluate students was appalling. I shared the results with Al and his retort was "I'm not surprised. Some of these liberally educated people have no allegiance to any thing or anybody. They tend to be biased against public campuses even where journalism was taught." He shrugged. "A few don't even know the kind of readers who subscribe to their own papers."

A few told me it was my job to grade students! I accepted that, obviously, because it was my duty even though in some instances I had to do my own review so the student could get a grade. Several said they didn't have enough details to make judgments. A number said they didn't have time! At the same time, they agreed to the task that cost students expensive tuition hours at their own expense.

My response was that this was a coordinated task; the newspaper or broadcast station took a person who was a journalism major who wanted to understand more about the work, transport themselves sometimes daily to the plant or station without reimbursement or pay. They were interested enough to want to find out more about it.

Al liked the idea.

I saw and heard gender difficulties, racial discrimination, the worst form of elitism I had witnessed in my young career, the most careless system of record-keeping I had seen since the Army and total disregard for respect of a young person or older person (as more veterans and older women in particular) entered the marketplace. At the same time, I saw students who needed career guidance flounder. Back then, few media outlets had human resources departments. In fact, the words "human resources" weren't in the lexicon. Editors still had an image of the movie "Front Page," I think.

Al replied: "Welcome back to America, Jack, now you see what's happened to our country. Media, like doctors, are slow to accept change. I think we're making progress but it's long process. Nobody welcomed me back and I assume they didn't cheer you either." This was 1969, not 2016.

In classes he strengthened what those of who were teaching about news work emphasized. "I wasn't happy with what I found when I took over at Gannett. But I had seen the same thing elsewhere. Degrees didn't make reporters," he laughed, and smiled again when I agreed with him.

He believed in what I was doing at UC. Four years after we met, I got a call from the president of the college who asked me come to his office "Right away!"

The college president and I had a good relationship but you always react with that Chicken Little response: what did I do wrong now...is the sky falling?

"How well do you know Al Neuharth?" the president asked. "Very well. He's been here and knows what we're doing. Why?"

"The Gannett Foundation has given the UC Journalism program $250,000 in Gannett stock for scholarships! Great work!" the president replied. That was 20 scholarships the first two or three years! Gannett later gave the college another $250,000 for the library which is now called the Frank E. Gannett Library.

It allowed us to give more than 20 scholarships a year for the last two decades I was on the campus.

Like all doers, Al was disliked by some in the backbiting world of media. He was considered brash, blunt and, at times, autocratic.

To me? Al Neuharth was an outstanding journalist, publisher and communicator. Equally important, he was a good friend.

He made his mark in American journalism by establishing a great experiment in journalism, USA TODAY. In 1982 it became the third most widely read paper.

I've worked for three Gannett papers, a Charles Sawyer paper, Harry Truman's Secretary of Commerce; the Associated Press, CBS, PBS, helped establish the English language broadcasting service in Korea, organized the broadcast station for President Vere Bird in Antigua and several family newspapers as well as one in my own family. I started a magazine called Home Business along with good friend, art designer and talented creative guru, Steve Lisi.

*Al Neuharth.*   Wikipedia

Al helped build Gannett from a regional publishing firm to a worldwide enterprise. By 1979, Gannett owned 78 daily papers, 21 weeklies, seven TV stations and more than 12 radio outlets. It became the largest newspaper company in the US. In addition, he purchased outdoor advertising plants and bought Harris & Associates to do the research necessary to determine the feasibility of launching USA Today.

Equally important, he took what once was the Gannett Foundation and renamed it the Freedom Foundation and served as chairman from 1991 until his death, 2013. In 2010, he started a weekly column called which "Plain Talk."

Plain talk from a newspaper man who believed that such "talk" was necessary. I think about my old friend when I read his column in my new hometown the Port St Lucie News Tribune.

# Jimmy Carter
## A different kind of White House

The difference between Jimmy Carter and Ronald Reagan was simple: the size of the government.

While Reagan preferred and fought hard for a smaller federal government, Carter preferred a larger national one requiring more space enough, buildings and personnel. Both men, however, wanted to help people. Carter believed that government could, if managed correctly, give people opportunity and growth. Reagan, of course, believed self-initiative and growth created better answers.

Funny thing is both thought government was a tool. However, the devil, as in so many situations, is in the details. Carter believed, for example, the government could protect land from abuse while Reagan argued for private use and ownership of land was the best for all concerned.

But Carter also added more expense. He created the Department of Education and more jobs for women and minorities. He spearheaded a move to get both houses of Congress to pass an energy bill and create an urgency for conservation of natural resources. Through his efforts Congress also approved the appointment of the first secretary of Energy in 1977. His choice? Republican James R. Schlesinger, a Nixon appointee who had switched his support of from President Jerry Ford to Carter in 1976. Schlesinger, of Arlington, VA, strongly advocated nuclear power and he was disillusioned by the Democratic Party's endorsement of California Gov. Jerry Brown's policies on foreign affairs and energy.

Schlesinger, together with Carter and others, took on Jane Fonda and her followers after a Washington rally that attempted to replace the new secretary of energy. "Putting Schlesinger in charge of nuclear power is like putting Dracula in charge a blood bank," Gov. Jerry Brown of California told the crowd of nearly 65,000 activists.

Said Schlesinger in response: "These are the same people who were for Ho Chi Minh."

Jim Schlesinger was one of the first persons I met when I was asked to interview Jimmy Carter. I was working for US Oil Week as a correspondent and the editor was interested in two things; Schlesinger's oil background and his faith.

Strange, I thought, I'm going to do a story on an energy chief and couple that with a story about his faith. I found out why shortly after we met. Schlesinger grew up in a middle class German Jewish family. A visit to West Germany in 1950, he told me, caused him to revisit his view of what he believed in. "I was a 'Calvinist' who found my German heritage so linked to the Lutheran faith, I became a Lutheran," he told me. "It is a major branch of Protestantism and it strongly affirms the theology that says Christ and the Holy Spirit together with God form the Triune God."

## JIMMY CARTER

He graduated from Harvard the same year he went to Germany. He was one of the more conservative members of a class that included former Secretary of State Henry Kissinger, Nixon's cabinet member and celebrated writer and performer George Plimpton. "We had good discussions occasionally," he smiled. "Rarely agreed, but that was what college was to do...give you a variety of opinions," he added.

President Carter worked to expand the National Parks System and protection of 103 million acres of Alaskan lands. He had difficulty presenting his case even to Democrats. Gas prices were climbing around the country and Carter was attempting to limit the amount of exploration and use of existing of oil fields. Critics believed it would make the fuel problem in America more severe but Carter listened to his energy chief who drafted legislation that ended natural gas price controls and levied a tax on gas-guzzling vehicles. He was criticized for limiting American free choice. Schlesinger was unsympathetic.

*Jimmy Carter 39th president*   White House photo

Carter's military tenure of seven years as a Naval officer in nuclear submarines and superior education seemed to make it more difficult for him to deal with politicians on a grass roots level with personal relationships especially in international affairs. Jimmy was a '46 graduate of the US Naval Academy at Annapolis, MD where undoubtedly he got to see and examine the western Maryland home of Camp David and he saw the beauty of the Catoctin countryside.

He was considered somewhat aloof, many said, which was probably one of the reasons he had some problems understanding the Russians who were gregarious to a fault. It was something, I think, in talking to several of his aides, he misunderstood. The complexities of the language and the meaning of interpretations—even with interpreters— could be vexing to anyone highly educated or not. American presidents have had that problem since George Washington and will more than likely continue to do so. He wasn't generally involved in international politics thus he had to rely on aides primarily he brought from Georgia in the beginning.

Like every administration I witnessed, personalities rise and fall in short months not years and anyone who has worked in DC knows that it takes time to not only know the right people but the people in right agencies. A long time secretary was frequently the best and more knowledgeable person within a staff. That didn't always sit well with new personnel who liked to deal with titles and "assume" such persons knew the ropes. Jimmy made that "very clear" to the world in his State of the Union speech in January, 1980, when he announced the Carter Doctrine.

On domestic matters, Carter worked to expand the National Parks System and the protection of 103 million acres of protected Alaskan lands. He had some difficulties making that case to all Democrats. Gas prices continued climbing around the country and the president attempted to explain how exploration would go forward as before and the use of existing oil fields would be curtailed at the same time. Critics believed both would make fuel prices keep going up and production drop. But Carter listened to his new energy chief who drafted legislation to end natural gas price controls and leveled a tax on gas-guzzling vehicles. He was criticized for limiting American free choice. But tried to hold his position.

He was a very disciplined man of great Christian faith. He demonstrated it many times over his four years. He continues to do so. The former president has also continued to teach Sunday School and Bible classes in his hometown of Plains, GA when in town. He is known as a man of principle and strong beliefs. I admire him for that. My father was very much like that.

A lifelong Democrat, he surprised many when newspaper and television reports said he had not voted for Presidential candidate Hilary Clinton in the fall, 2016, presidential election. He supported Vermont's Bernie Sanders instead, if media reports were correct. If accurate, that surprised me.

At one press conference I attended I overheard Jimmy tell an aide that with "unemployment reaching 8 percent there was no way for the country to live" with such an outlay of federal dollars. He found himself moving closer to Harry Truman when he agreed with several cabinet members that FDR's famous "fireside chats" might offer a reasonable way to explain a different approach. The TV chats showed Jimmy in front of a fireplace relaxing wearing a sweater and talking to ordinary Americans in town meetings. He even stayed overnight with a few of the families to gain the "people support" which political pollster Pat Cadell suggested would show his public support. A few months after it started, it ceased because an overwhelmed Secret Service couldn't protect the president at various locations. It also didn't meet the goal sought.

Carter wanted success where others, Democrats and Republicans, had tried and came up short.

Quite similar to today's lack of bipartisanship or discussions across the two parties, he didn't appear to have the temperament or patience to get opposite members of the two bodies to really enter into constructive talks.

Carter's plan, for example, to help households and families nationally by giving people a $50 tax rebate to stimulate the economy passed the House but was rejected by the Senate. He felt betrayed, like so many presidents, when he clearly let congressmen and women see he would not become a part of a larger government spending machine.

Furthermore, he became the first president since WW II to propose that a new position, Secretary of Energy, be added to the cabinet.

I remember talking to Camp David crew members about the transition from the Ford family to the Carters. "The change from the Reagans to the Fords, who were only in the White House for two years, was delightful, I was told. You were dealing with young people primarily, who enjoyed doing things and being outside. The Reagans, of course, loved horseback riding and walking in the wooded area around the camp. The Carters loved walking in the woods. The Carters probably walked farther than the Reagans and they swam in the Aspen pool. Jimmy and Rosalyn bowled at the two lanes available at

*Presidents Gerald Ford, Richard Nixon, George Herbert Walker Bush, Ronald Reagan and Jimmy Carter*
Whitehouse Photo

the Hickory Lodge and, like their predecessors, the Reagans, enjoyed movies."

Betty Ford loved to tell the story about the beautifully prepared, tasty food at Camp David. Staffers chuckled when they heard the Fords describe the great cuisine at the camp. Several noted the glances between Rosalyn and Jimmy when talking about food. Both were smiling. The Carters were very clearly weight conscious environmentalists and early to bed types. "It's going to be different. Much different," one camp veteran mused.

*Jimmy and Rosalynn Carter on a road at Camp David*
(courtesy of Jimmy Carter Library)

The Fords and Carters shared one common thread during their tenures at the camp. Both couples were scrupulously thrifty when it came to budgeting, camp regulars said of the way the Fords and the Carters scrupulously kept careful track of purchases and guest expenditures. The Kennedys and the Nixons, I discovered, never gave cost much of a thought. Rosalyn and Betty, it seemed, took on the family spending ... and were frugal. Pat Nixon, it was said by the staffer I talked with, let husband Richard deal with the finances.

The Carters were eager to visit Camp David from the time they won the election in 1977. They had loved the open, rustic nature that surrounded the site at Thurmont, MD. Unlike other presidents they vowed to visit once a month. They kept their commitment. My hunch is Annapolis, which wasn't far away, gave them the opportunity to explore the territory. But inside the electrified fence that surrounds the mountain acreage, the cabins, called lodges originally, were updated continually after Mamie Eisenhower's approval in 1958 to renovate the compound. The changes began when a detachment of Seabees showed up to assist the camp by draining the septic tank in front of the commander's lodge.

A staff member told me that the crew was there to relieve a sewage problem that had plagued the camp and has been fixed. A engineer assigned to drain the septic tank in front of the commander's lodge.

A young engineer was assigned the task and probably wished he hadn't. The spot had been a problem for years, former Camp administrator Bill King explained. "I told him he had two possible choices: 1. Redo the drain field or 2. Run the line down the hill to the system that served Aspen ( main lodge)." King told the Seabee engineer that "he would have to dig the trench by hand because a backhoe would tear up too much grass and kill a lot of trees." He messed it up.

When the commander came back to inspect the work "he went nuts," King laughed. "He was so angry he confined the young engineer to quarters!"

The Carters were so excited by the chance to visit the Cactocton retreat that they visited a month after their inauguration in February, 1977. They were accompanied by Chip and Caron Carter and Jeff and Annette Carter and daughter Amy. They took a Marine helicopter to the secret hideaway.

Mrs. Lillian (president's mother) visited the camp for the first time in July 1977 and the extended family wanted to attend church services. Carter thought the church program should be held at Camp David and arrangements were hastily made at Hickory Lodge Theater to hold a church service. Staff found a military field alter and the chaplain at nearby Fort Richie, MD provided hymnals for the family. Jimmy had his first service as he wanted it, at Camp David, the government retreat.

# Lyndon B. Johnson

## He excited young voters

I was just back from my military service as a correspondent for the Pacific Stars & Stripes working for my hometown paper, the Lancaster Eagle Gazette in central Ohio and the country was getting ready to help Lyndon Johnson heal the wounds caused by the death of popular President Jack Kennedy by assassination in Dallas.

Johnson offered America what he called a "Great Society" which was a collection of Democratic thoughts from former New Deal brain trust people and some newcomers from Texas.

When I became a Pacific Stars & Stripes correspondent (while still a member of the US Army assigned in Korea) I was able to use my position to help provide a flow of solid news and features about what I felt were stories of interest to my new audience among Far East readers.

The military showed me just how poorly government can handle any issue regarding the public whether health, military or taxes. Careless without feeling is the best description I can offer. I remember a Black sergeant at Fort Hood, TX said it best with his Georgian drawl: "I ain't your momma or your daddy, got that?"

I felt that the country and my wife and I deserved a "great society."

I was determined to write a story that the S&S wouldn't publish because of repercussions of higher command. It took me two or three years back in the states to finally sell it freelance. It was one of my reasons for turning down S&S to continue my career although I was offered a good position.

A PT boat had sunk in the smelly Han River and had been refloated by a team of Navy contractors and Seabees and refurbished at US government expense I was told. The crew put a new coat of paint on it and the military brass began bringing groups of influential congressmen, wives and Korean dignitaries to parties on board. Wine, liquor and excellent cuisine flowed and was consumed. I remembered going past it in the last month or two of my tour of duty. I wasn't invited to the parties because it wasn't in my sector of coverage at the time. But I saw enough to tell me that taxpayers should know about it. I talked to several legislators when I got back home about what I saw and thought. One I asked was President Johnson. I didn't remember that he was a Navy officer. He laughed and said had I tried to get that story published I probably would have been charged with "something" because it was an "internal matter." The vessel was labeled the "Korean Party Barge," I found out later.

Johnson appealed to all of us because he was offering a new way forward. It created excitement and it appeared to be what a demoralized country sought. Yet, he and his deputies were trying to control the lunge ahead.

# LYNDON BAINES JOHNSON

At the same time, Lyndon Johnson demonstrated a lack of civility and a personal elitism that were repugnant to me. I saw it so many times in my years as a journalist. It used to eat at me. I learned to disregard it and burrow deeper in the issue. Lyndon, to me, was like so much of our history, bluster, bombast and little action. A gentle memo with no teeth would be sent instead. From Thomas Jefferson to Barack Obama we've witnessed such innuendo and misdirection. Read letters, memoranda and notes from presidents and aides and agency directors state and federal libraries and repositories and you can put together more than the final documents reveal. It has long legs in American discourse and offers no conclusions just creates more questions. The Johnson era was filled with such turmoil. I saw it close up and from a distance.

However, I thought Johnson's suggestions were what America needed. I even was motivated to return to the Democratic Party and volunteer to help organize for future events. I attended an organizational meet-

*Lyndon B. Johnson 36th president*   White House photo

ing when LBJ came to Columbus, OH. I listened to several speakers and then asked my question about the party barge. He scowled and mumbled that he knew nothing about it. I pressed him.: What do you want to know pissant?" He hissed that he had answered the question. Next?

Lyndon Johnson, America's 36th president, was brash, at times, an uncontrolled personality. At 6'4," he towered over many he met and he made people feel uncomfortable because he gave blank stares or a scowl and didn't always respond until a pause had become very pregnant. A number of presidential aides said that was the way he processed things.

Smart but crafty, I thought. That's why he was where he was. Though each president used similar methods, the process was made more precarious because of the vanities you encountered. Johnson, I noted, felt the office gave him God like authority. His presence, image and the way he intimidated aides and others enhanced that persona. That's a basic flaw in the way Americans are forced to see the presidency. Media have much to do with it. Like a CEO, not like a participant in governing a vast bureaucracy. Even Johnson's predecessor recognized limits and the caution needed in dealing with all parts of the infrastructure. God bless the founding fathers for their wisdom.

I spent some time in 1974 following the president on the campaign trail. When I attended one or two of his stops in West Virginia and Kentucky, for example, his exuberant but coarse language in that slurpy twang, didn't always explain his very over-simplifications of Vietnam, civil rights, a new "great society" and budgetary issues, I felt.

I was, of course, working for a Democratic newspaper in a conservative region of the state. Our city reporter who covered politics was a knowledgeable guy who made sure that he covered all his bases. In a city like Lancaster where advertising was mostly local industry and small business, owner Charles Sawyer, a Cincinnati lawyer by trade and personality, wasn't one who would invest in major area causes.

Yes, he supported the Red Cross and the local Salvation Army but he wasn't about to give support to building a new stadium for the public high school football team. That's a bridge too far. Much to far. I'm sure Mr. Sawyer thought that it would possibly hurt local advertising revenue. I was told that the sports editor I replaced was fired because he didn't heed good advice. In many Ohio cities, football was more important than politics.

Funny about that, President Johnson heard our discussion and turned to me and said : "You could do so much better than this in a bigger community. You're like a fish out of water here," he added and then recognized the "pissant" he had dealt with some months earlier. Unfortunately, he said it in front of media colleagues (not friends). I explained to my editor that the president knew I had an American history-journalism degree and he wanted to know why I wasn't teaching. I let it drop not wanting to show my hand. Poker is not only a game of skill it's an acquired part of daily life. I had learned political savvy in the military that continues to this day.

I spent several hours observing the president with Job Corps campers at Camp David shortly after he was in the White House. I was diverted from Camp David down the road to Job Corps Center. I drove through a security screen that asked for my ID. I used my expired military pass. It worked. I doubt if it would today.

Pres. Lyndon B. Johnson meets with advisors in Aspen Lodge at Camp David
LBJ Library photo by Yoichi Okamoto

He seemed to enjoy the questions he got at the Job Corps Center. He spent so much time there, aides said, he was very late for the briefing with military and foreign affairs specialists at Camp David. He stayed for dinner and then returned for Washington. He was disturbed, I noted, by the demonstrations at the White House. However, he continued to say that he preferred his ranch to Camp David. One of the reporters standing with me said under his breath "that's because getting to his ranch is much more difficult than getting into Camp David."

Pres. Lyndon B. Johnson with advisors Amb. Ellsworth Bunker and Amb. Averell Harriman at Camp David
LBJ Library photo by Yoichi Okamoto

While he didn't care for Camp David, the family seemed to love their escapes to visit the Thurmont location. "They were happy to go there and all of us shared that feeling," he told me. I remembered when I did my book on Camp David that he told me that his daughter Lynda Johnson had visited Harriet Chapel at Catocton Furnace to go to church. The family attended services at Camp David.

## LYNDON BAINES JOHNSON

The family, including Lyndon, loved to walk on the paths at the camp. In April, 1968, after making the difficult decision not to seek re-election, he took the familiar short flight from Washington to Thurmont to relax. He reported in his book Vantage Point "I flew to...Camp David. It was a relief to get away from the noise and carbon monoxide of downtown Washington. At the Aspen Lodge, I changed into more comfortable clothes and sat in the living room talking with Walt Rostow (a senior advisor) about the problems we would be discussing the next day. Finally, I dozed off in my chair until dinnertime. The next morning, I drove to the helicopter pad to greet my visitors from Washington. We went to the Lodge and over breakfast, talked about Vietnam and the latest exchanges with Hanoi. We moved outside to enjoy the sunshine." It was his last note on the camp.

As complex as he was combative, Johnson could show genuine feeling about people. He remembered several young men at the Job Corps Center when I was there and said "I hope it leads to good opportunities for them. I know what that can be like," he sighed.

History courses over the years have avoided telling us much about such interactions between presidents and citizens young and old. I'm not sure why although as a teacher there are so many important things to discuss in class you're hard pressed to get it all in without making the course boring with details within an hour.

There was another more compassionate side to Lyndon Johnson, too. It showed at the Edmund Pettus Bridge in Selma, AL when white law officers stopped a peaceful march by John Lewis and Hosea Williams and the marchers knelt to pray. Officers fired tear gas and began to beat them. President John F. Kennedy had been assassinated in Dallas and the new president was back in DC gathering his thoughts about what to tell an anxious nation about what was ahead. As he left Air Force One on that chilly November night, he told a small crowd near the tarmac: "I ask for your help—and God's"—he said exhausted from the experience.

## LYNDON BAINES JOHNSON

A deputy press aide in the White House answered my call for the Associated Press for a response to what had happened in Alabama and he replied "The president was most upset. He wants people to know that will not be the way we go forward."

Said former Newsweek Editor Jon Meacham in his excellent book American Gospel that when the president discovered his national speech was being written by someone he didn't know, "Johnson sat upright, his voice raised in sudden anger...'I don't need a Texas public relations man! Get Dick (Goodwin, his speech writer) to do it. And now!'"

Lyndon Johnson demanded that his orders be carried out IMMEDIATELY!

I know from my own brief experience with him, Johnson didn't tolerate "slow response." Immediate meant IMMEDIATE! Several aides told me if you worked in his White House in press relations you were a First Responder for whatever time it took. Having worked under such pressure on deadline for 10 years with the Associated Press and previously Pacific Stars & Stripes, you realized the different unwritten rules of the workplace.

Goodwin said when he arrived at the White House within hours that horrendous weekend, the president was still angry and coming off a "long liquid dinner party at the house of Arthur Schlesinger Jr. in Washington."

He was at the his typewriter within minutes, typing paper and fresh morning air were all he needed. "It just came to me," he told Meachem. Johnson was virtually waiting for each page. He wanted to see what could shown listeners how the country wasn't waiting. It was moving ahead ...and on track. I had written such comments using my daily log of 24 hour commentary by US and even world leaders on events in releases for an Ohio congressman and later, several candidates for office from New York.

Meachem wrote: "The biblical imagery is part of the American tradition, no matter what your personal beliefs are, the Old Testament, the New Testament, is all woven into who we are Christian, Jew, or whatever. Religious metaphors and religious language for a kind of common bond in America. That's what the speech unfolded trying to replicate FDR's Fireside chats in WWII," Goodwin explained.

Johnson told Americans with as much emotion as a Texan could use "I speak tonight for the dignity of man and the democracy. We shall overcome."

"We will guard against violence, knowing it strikes from our hands the very weapons which we seek—progress, obedience to law and belief in American values," he continued in his thick Texas accent. He spoke slowly when in front of a microphone or on TV to protect himself from using a swear word that too frequently would slip into conversation with an aide or others publicly. A good number

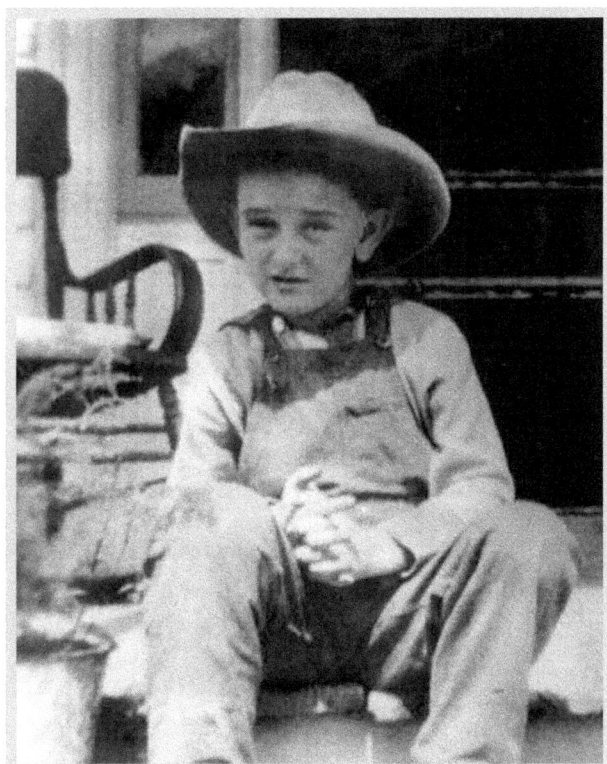

*Lyndon Johnson in 1915 at his family home in the Texas*
Wikimedia

of public officials including presidents had that problem regardless of their faith and church affiliation.

Presidents Eisenhower, Truman, Kennedy were aware of their use of obscenities and tried to edit themselves. All failed and relied on news media to help them edit much of it. At a public affair with Johnson I was told to turn off my mike just after a rant in which he called others names and took the Lord's name in vain so many times I realized there was less news and far more profanity than anything usable. I ended up with less than a page of information.

US Postage stamp: LBJ, 1973    Wikimedia

During my time in news work, such language was far more obvious mostly from men speakers. Much depended on the audience but when feminists came on the scene, it seemed, in my opinion, to grow more intense. I attribute it and today to lack of self-discipline then manners or décor. The argument overcame self-control. It got worse as speakers realized they frequently got more attention "letting their hair down" as those of us reporting discovered. If you remember the 1960s you know how bad it got and the FCC didn't really interfere unless public safety was an issue.

The Johnsons had a great time with longtime friends Prime Minister Harold Holt and his wife from Australia. They spent time together as they had done a number of times watching home movies involving family and friends at Camp David. On Sundays when they were at the retreat, they went to church service and usually with about 15 staff members too.

Lyndon visited a number of times without Lady Bird. He visited Camp David, for example, 20 times in his five years and six months. Said a longtime staff member who is still on the crew, "I only remember once when Lady Bird was with the president."

There are several large fireplaces in camp and they put out a great deal of smoke especially if they are not used almost daily and tended to. I used to lay logs on the fires and the rooms would get very hot. Mrs. Johnson would invariably ask the staff for the dining room table to be moved closer to the fire," he said. Absolutely a mistake in those cabins!" he laughed. "It would get unbelievably hot!"

Then there was the time, the staffer told me, when the president called a "red alert" in the camp. One of his secretaries was missing. Lyndon had called for her during the day shortly after she arrived. She didn't respond.

Johnson was noticeably agitated as he bound from his office in Aspen Cabin and shouted out to a puzzled security guard to "Close the gate! Don't let anyone out! Get a search party together! Find her!"

A platoon of Marines did begin a search of nearby trails. An hour later they had little result. Then, the woman appeared coming slowly down a back trail absentmindedly walking with some flowers she found.

Those were the ups and downs in the Johnson Administration.

# BILL CLINTON

## Like all presidents, likeable Bill Clinton was flawed

I met Bill Clinton, then governor of Arkansas, months before he stepped on to a national stage that for eight years gave him luster and tarnish at the same time.

We met in the governor's office in Little Rock where I had journeyed with a poor road map and no GPS (not available in those days) or Smart Phone to help me travel from Huntington, WVA to Little Rock. It was, in fact, a horrible trip. I had a room in a small motel a few miles away. It was a hot dry southwest day when I got to his office in the capitol. His secretary was out for lunch but the door was open. I walked in and this good looking, tall but well proportioned man looked up from his desk and got up with a big smile and drawled "How you doing?"

"Hot," I said with my own smile. "Where are you from?" he said. Originally from Ohio but now teaching at Marshall in Huntington, I replied.

"A good school. I remember watching them in a semi-final NCAA game. They looked good," he added. I introduced myself and started to explain my purpose when his secretary appeared and asked if I was Prof. John Behrens. We all laughed at the secretary's attempt to explain where she was. "We're both ok with your lunch break," Bill smiled. I warmed up to a guy I felt I could relate to.

I got into my purpose for the trip to Little Rock.

"Governor, the plans you propose for reforming education, do they include college and graduate school too?"

"Of course," he replied quickly. "But we know that the lower schools are in desperate need for changes now. It's a problem here and elsewhere. It's not one state that isn't while others are moving ahead. At the same time, we have to have a plan that encompasses all. What do you think?"

I told him from what I see, it's a good idea. I told him I have student teachers in my classes and they aren't happy with the kinds of requirements that they feel are unnecessary. "Were you happy with all the classes you took outside your major?" he inquired with a laugh.

"No, sir," I smiled in return. "But I think that if we offer student teachers a chance to experiment under supervision it could be more flexible for all, what do you think about that?" I responded. He thought for several minutes and then looked at me more carefully and replied "And how would senior faculty ---full professors--- see that?"

"Probably as a threat to their turf," I told him. "Which says that we would have a battle before we got anything off the ground," he said shrugging.

## BILL CLINTON

"How do you plan to do that at Marshall?" he asked me. "It's an old school with solid people and students who want to learn, but," I told him "Over time I want to introduce internships at the sophomore and junior years not last semester seniors type of plan," I explained. He thought for a minute or two. "It could work especially in your field," he smiled.

His secretary interrupted and said that his 2:30 appointment with the Attorney General was here and "you have to review some documents before you meet with him," she whispered. I took the hint as time to leave. "Thanks for your time. I enjoyed our conversation," I told him.

We shook hands as he gathered up the papers on his desk and started for the door. He was affable and polite and when I saw him again briefly in Washington we exchanged smiles from a distance. I was attending one of the early press conferences for incoming President George W. Bush.

Bill Clinton was the youngest person---at 46---since John F. Kennedy to become president. He had been the youngest governor of Arkansas too. I sent him several letters asking him to answer a few more questions. He never responded. As a working musician with a union card I wanted to know how he dealt with the urge to play when he entered politics. A press aide sent me a cryptic note saying that "the president continues to play for fun and his own enjoyment."

When I researched and wrote the book Camp David I asked several members of the staff about the president's leisure hours when he visited. "Depending upon the time of season, he was either pleasant or cranky. You know he had allergies and that told the story really," I was told.

Clinton was criticized throughout his two terms at the White

## BILL CLINTON

House by veterans' groups and women. His opposition to the Vietnam War was fueled by his lack of military service while others his age were being drafted. Though he used a number of legitimate deferments, the rising casualty rate from the war was no small matter to parents and servicemen.

A Rhoades Scholar, he tried to explain he was in England which didn't pacify many. When Whitewater surfaced as a campaign problem, he faced more heat from media. Questions and charges of fraud about a real estate deal that failed became of personal involvement and a number of political friends, (a few went to jail) the Clintons were never indicted. They emerged bruised but unscathed. Political operatives I knew in Washington said his youthful face and innocent look to the camera eye were quite effective. However, things got much worse as the months went by.

His famous reply "I did not have sexual relations with that woman" echoed in discussions everywhere when he tried to defend a sordid affair with Monica Lewinsky, a 22-year-old assistant which brought on an impeachment charge .

The House of Representatives voted to impeach and two-thirds of House members voted to remove him from office Dec. 19, 1995. The charge was perjury. The Senate, however, voted 50 -50 on the obstruction charge and thus acquitted the president.

Yet, during his eight years in office, even his opponents agreed he had brought economic success in the very early days of the 21st century. But the failure of universal health care was attributed to both Clintons because of a flawed plan they supported.

He tried to use Camp David to woo Palestinians and Jews to settle their centuries-old issues. Once again, the two sides refused to end the dispute although both sides agreed the US was a vital partner in their negotiations. But Bill Clinton left office with more popularity than later Democratic candidate, Barack Obama, America's 44th president. A 2010 NBC and Wall Street Journal poll found that Clinton was more popular than Obama by a 55 to 46 percent rating. Clinton was able to bring the rising crime rate to a 26 year low by the time he ended two terms. He also raised US education standards by distributed $2 billion in assistance. His 1994 America School Act received support from Democrats and Republicans as well as business and education communities.

*Bill Clinton tried to use Camp David to woo Palestinians and Jews to settle their centuries-old issues.* White House photo

Every president and his wife felt the need, it seems, to redecorate Camp David. While presidents could use the retreat, each seemed to feel the need to add personal touches whether needed or not.

The Roosevelts, because of budget constraints of an eminent war, took a very modest approach. FDR decided to use second hand chairs from Naval warehouse storage and some of his own drawings and paintings on the walls. Jack Kennedy made sure his rocker was in place to help with a bad back and Jackie added riding trails at the camp. Mamie Eisenhower, who most believe was responsible for most of the changes in the early years of modernization of Camp David hired Harold Grieve. Ronald and Nancy Reagan brought in Ted Grabor from California .

The Bushes got help from designer Mark Hampton while Bill and Hilary Clinton chose Little Rock, AR interior designer Karl Hocker-

*Camp David swimming pool.*   White House photo

smith to redecorate the off- limits public retreat. The Clintons added a swimming pool, a tennis court, and a jogging track to the White House compound and Camp David. The US taxpayer paid for all the changes.

I played Camp David twice, once with President Clinton and once with President Reagan. We weren't allowed to keep score with President Clinton ( I scribbled a 3 (par) on that foursome. With President Reagan I again scored a par 3. I used a 7 iron and a putter. Camp David staff warned us that to divulge our scores would cancel any future playing dates.

According to David McCullough in his book, *Power and Presidency* edited by Robert A. Wilson, 1999, the entertainment budget for the president was $12,000 with a travel budget of $100,000. I'm sure that has been changed but no one in the White House offers an answer.

President Clinton left office contending that more work was still to be done.

# RONALD REAGAN
## Meeting the President for Lunch

My meeting with President Ronald Reagan on July 12, 1985 was prearranged by a man who became a friend, although we never met face to face until years later. Director of Communications, Pat Buchanan, was the voice on the phone who created the noon meeting.

Washington was hotter than Florida in the summer and I dressed to meet it. Even then, I sweltered with White House air conditioning groaning to meet 70 degrees!

Around the table with me in the Old West Wing of the White House were other editors and broadcasters and White House staffers at the time.

Besides Pat and Larry Speakes, another presidential deputy press secretary, Marlin Fitzwater, press secretary to then Vice Presi-

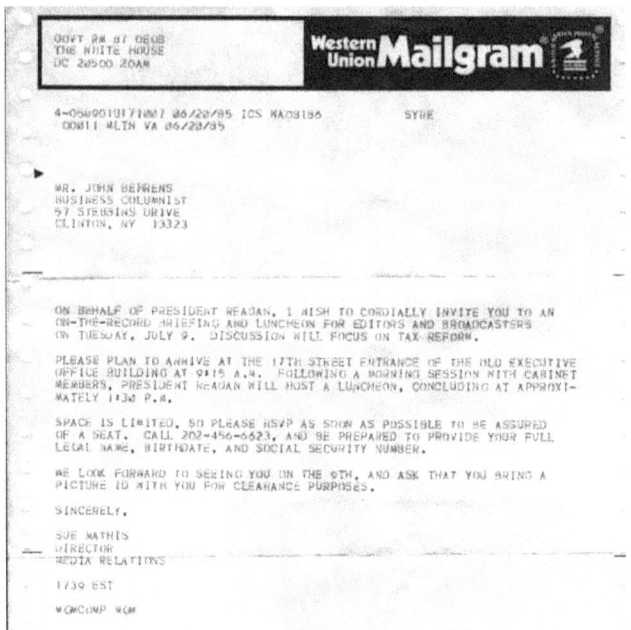

*Jack's personal invitation to on the record briefing with President Reagan*

dent George H.W Bush, and Linda Chavez, director of the Office of Public Liaison, a mixture of editors and staff aides surrounded us at other tables. Linda, I suspected, had been part of the planning team to devise this new approach to reach the Middle American media that wasn't normally invited to the White House. It was one of the efforts that I applauded President Reagan for instituting to reach a public that was generally ignored for decades. At the time, I was reaching an estimated 6 million Americans and foreign readers in Elks, Home Business, and Canadians in American Printer. I had a good number of South Africans and Black printers who liked my humor; they told me in letters the AP sent on to me. Odd but true and I never knew how that developed.

"A good warm afternoon to you," President Reagan began with a broad smile.

"We wanted to give you a taste of the nation's capitol at a time of the year when you're planning vacations in cooler surroundings so you would understand what it's like here." Laughter greeted his humor.

The all Black wait staff was the most personable and accommodating I had experienced at such an affair. I told him so. He smiled and said "thank you for all of us" and filled my water glass.

The President got right to the point. "Turning to the tax plan (it was being argued in Congress that year) when the income tax became law back in 1913 the tax code came to 15 pages. Today (1985) it adds up to 4 volumes and more than 4,000 pages. It requires some 6 feet of shelf space and weighs almost 90 pounds," he added with amusement. The "complexity is staggering. The injustice is worse." Things certainly haven't changed!

*Reagan's White House Luncheon Menu*

Courtesy Ronald Reagan Library

Reagan's staff decided to get more middle American editors, writers and columnists involved with what was, for years, not as covered live or in detail as current day's Washington decision-making. There were few cable news outlets then.

The Carter Administration failed during the preceding weeks of summer, 1985, to secure the release of government embassy staff members from a sovereign government (Iran). Instead, the hostages were forceably imprisoned by a mob and dealt with in a ruthless manner.

Carter tried everything within his power but didn't have the status in world politics to create such a way to affect our shaky world at that time. The "spokes of the wheel" approach to government, said Chris Whipple in his 2017 book, "The Gatekeepers," wasn't working. Carter had stubbornly refused to appoint a chief of staff for his White House. It cost him friends in a Washington that still operated by traditional rules. That was demonstrated when President Carter had a cabinet shake up and asked the entire group to resign. The public and the media were led to believe the worst and see little hope in what the government was doing to free innocent government workers in a foreign country doing their jobs.

Carter never overcame that impression. It took the election of President Reagan to free Americans. We briefly talked about how perceptions played a part in some of Reagan's methodology at that time. Jim Baker, who was sitting close by overheard what the President said and nodded his head in agreement. Carter didn't have the ability to use humor to deflect and lighten serious discussion. He wasn't much of a conversationalist, I noted this from attending a few of his press conferences years before. Reagan paid attention to details.

He stayed relaxed when dealing with difficult matters and pursued his course. It provided great dividends in his political posture and answers.

Courtesy Ronald Reagan Library

But he added further insights that day in July. He talked about his days playing football at Eureka College and even broadcasting the live games on radio station WHO, Des Moines, Iowa. "We were happy about a good clean block.

Courtesy Ronald Reagan Library

A good sharp tackle that stopped a runner. I never ever tried to injure anybody. That wasn't what the games were for or about! I just wanted to help my team score points and win the game. I think that's changed some what these days," he sighed.

"When I was on the radio, I put myself back there on the field. I let the listener feel the block with words and the tackles I watched on the field with pauses and groans that I felt for the players. I even put the mike outside the window so the audience could hear crowd reaction. If my timing was right, they could hear the hit itself."

I burst into his narrative to tell him I had the same feeling covering games at the Bowling Green State University stadium in Ohio. He laughed and then responded "Well I'm happy we didn't play you then. You had bigger players and the thuds were actually whacks that caused everyone to feel the pain instantly. Right?" I agreed with a shrug.

"The enjoyment was winning a game where playing was the fun. You enjoyed being a part of something that was successful. We we're not large guys you know. We were average sized—175 pounds or a few pounds more. It was rare to have a player 250 pounds then," he looked my way and laughed again. "I weighed 150 without the uniform," I retorted. Everybody started laughing. "See?" he continued. I enjoyed him.

Vice President President George H. Bush entered the room and took a seat. "We were talking about football, George," President Reagan continued. "Oh my, but the subject certainly fits, I think, Mr. President," Bush retorted.

*Reagan & Thatcher at Camp David.* Courtesy Ronald Reagan Library

"Let's face it," the President commented. "Our tax code has become 'un-American' and I mean that as a serious, moral and economic assertion. Americans are an expansive and optimistic people. We consistently seek opportunity and work to better ourselves." One more question? He asked.

"Mr. President, I have a great CD of you introducing Jimmy Dorsey and his Orchestra..." I began.

"Oh my, I remember those big band days and Nancy and I danced to so many. I'm glad you have some reminders of my experiences as your president...Thank you." He laughed.

I got a follow up note days later from Terry Abdoo, staff assistant, telling me that the President enjoyed sitting with me and he told Nancy about the commentary about Jimmy Dorsey because "Jimmy was a friend" from Hollywood times.

# PRESIDENT REAGAN

# Mr Clown

## God Bless You, Mr. Clown

The youngster laughed as the clown tweaked his nose. Suddenly his smile disappeared and the puzzled seven year old asked, "How can you be so happy in a wheelchair, Mr. Clown?"

The question has been asked again and again by children and adults who watched Ringling Brothers Barnum and Bailey Circus clown Happy Harry Sinclair perform. Confined to a wheelchair for a number of years, Happy refused to quit clowning. In fact, he entered into such new activities such as hospital shows, birthday parties and even donned his costume at several filling station impromptu performances.

Sadly, Ringling Brothers Barnum and Bailey Circus brought down the curtain for the final time in Riverdale, NY, in May 2017. One hundred and thirty-six years of great performances including those of my friend, Happy Harry Sinclair, from London, England, became memories cherished by those who saw him.

Grease pencil makeup and funny costumes concealed the pain, disappointment and hardship the 73-year-old entertainer endured privately from the time doctors told him that both of his legs would have to be amputated. "I couldn't hide it all the time . . . but I tried hard in front of the kids."

The removal of the limbs climaxed at three years of emergency trips to the hospital for treatment for diabetes and heart trouble. Though doctors didn't give Harry much hope, everyone underestimated his strong will to live and continue working.

"My belief in people, my faith in God and my trust in my doctors," he told me, "I knew all of them were working hard to save me and so I worked just as hard to help," he added with his jaunty smile. "I keep thinking to myself 'Harry Sinclair' there are many people who are in more pain than you in this hospital.' That's when I got thinking what I might do to help them and why I knew I had to get better."

The prospect of clowning from a wheelchair didn't interfere with Harry's plans. Although he knew that he wouldn't be able to travel with his circus friends again he started planning comedy routines for hospital wards and private parties especially for children. "I felt fit as a fiddle and doctors were en-

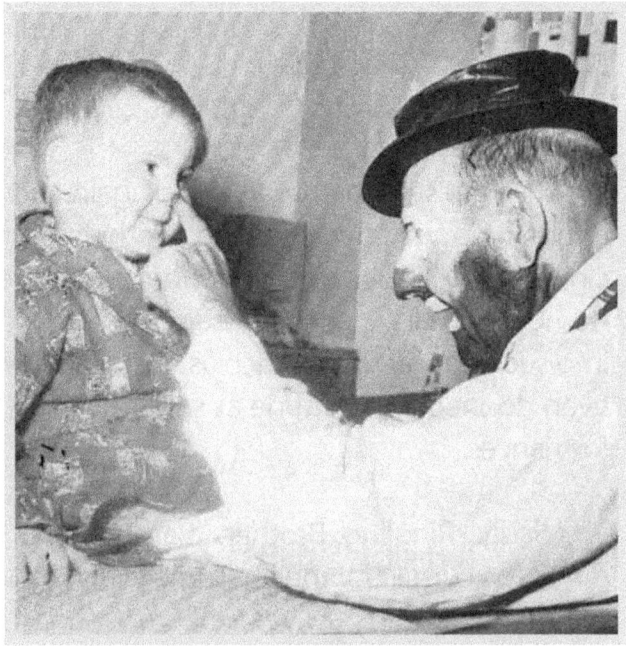

*Happy Sinclair, Ringling Brothers Barnum & Bailey Circus clown* Jack Behrens' Photo

couraging me, too." The applause from the shows generated more enthusiasm for the idea, the clown and the doctors.

"If you could see some of those smiling faces when they put those little arms up to you! Oh man, what a feeling it is when you see that grin develop or hear that belly laugh! Then, someone in the crowd says 'God bless you, Mr. Clown,' and you know that you've received your reward."

Happy saw smiles in every state in the union during his 20 years of traveling with the circus and ranked Maine and Massachusetts as the best places he played, with Ohio a close third. "People seem to really go all out for circuses in those areas especially," he remembered.

Before he became a bigtop performer he was better known as "Happy Harry the Flying Clown." When performing with the Howard Brothers Show in southern Ohio he would parachute from low flying planes and do aerial stunts such as climbing onto wings while in flight. "I made them laugh at the comical way I got on the wings and back in the planes," he reminisced.

He discovered it was more dangerous than he thought. "Once while we playing at a spot near a lake the wind took me off course and I hit the water three times before I went in. That smarted my bottom big time. The parachute jumps didn't bother me but there was a bigger problem; I don't swim a stroke!" he laughed.

A few years later, he had to ride a burning parachute to the ground. "There was about two feet of that darn thing left when I finally hit the dirt." He ended up in the hospital then with three fractured ribs from the fall. "I decided I had enough of that bloody thing with that jump."

An old hand in the days of slapstick on stage, Sinclair worked with some of the best in show business. His memories include engagements with Eddie Cantor, Al Jolson and the great clown, Emmett Kelly.

One of his fondest memories of Emmett, he says was at Madison Square Garden on the Gary Moore TV Show. Harry and Emmett's friendship led to other performances. But nothing, he said, topped a children's show they did later. It was an unrehearsed incident as the show started. "Emmett was to fire roman candles in the back of his pants as he entered the section where the kids were. Emmett jerked on the release to set the candles off too hard and they fell down his pants legs and started going off. I've never seen a man run so fast for a bucket of water to put a fire out in his pants!" It took more than an hour to get the show resumed. But the show went on. Emmett finished his routine!

His parents were both circus performers but the death of his mother, a high wire performer, was too much for his father. He retired to become a farmer in Maine a short while later.

Harry continued to perform at Lancaster Fairfield Hospital in Lancaster, OH where my first wife Patty, a Registered Dietitian, and a specialist on diabetes, worked with him. He died a few years later after we left the area.

The community showed its appreciation for the clown who came to town a stranger by making sure that he didn't have a pauper's funeral. The hospital, civic groups and others including my wife and I contributed to his burial expenses.

Harry became a part of my life too. At 84, I have remembered him as a good friend who inspired me to become a writer—"what a great thing to do and get paid too," he said--- and convince others as he did me "that you don't quit. Help others to find their way." His story hangs on my office wall as a reminder to me that God will tell you when your time is up.

# Chip Davis

## Was told too many times it couldn't be done

Like so many other successful entrepreneurs, composer Chip Davis avoided the advice of marketing gurus about his projects.

The result? His Mannheim Steamroller Christmas music CD was a smashing success. That was 1984. And Chip, who I interviewed in 1986, has been progressing along the music highway ever since.

It hasn't been an easy road, but it never is, he told me back then. "I wanted to do a Christmas album. Every retailer I talked to said it won't work out. So I did," he said in a typical Ohio matter of fact way.

The same thing happened when he produced and released his own production *Fresh Aire*.

"It started selling so well that regular retailers finally DID want it. I went ahead anyway. I did self promotion. I think, all in all, over its lifespan, we did well. I wrote the piece on *Fresh Aire* called 'Escape

From the Atmosphere.' In my mind I pictured a rocket taking off then releasing from gravity and traveling through space." He wrote a film score of that from what his mental image was of the object hurling into the unknown, he told Pollstar.

1984, the year George Orwell told us, in his book *1984*, could be the end of mankind as we knew it, was the year a 21st century composer created his success with musical scores from the 16th century.

"The name 'Mannheim Steamroller' came from the German musical technique in the 18th century called Mannheim roller (Mannheimer Waltze). It was a crescendo passage which contained a rising melodic line over an ostinato bass. It had been popularized by the Mannheim School of Composition in Germany.

A graduate of the University of Michigan and a member of the outstanding U of M marching band, Chip, a percussionist and bassoonist, remembers what it was like to find new ways to utilize melody and rhythm.

Chip came from a talented musical family in Hamler, OH. His father was a high school music teacher and his mother toured professionally with Phil Spitanly's All-Girl Orchestra. His grandmother taught him how to play piano.

"Sure, music has been a part of my life. And so has church music. Christmas carols were awesome I thought. I had a need to lift them to another level in my mind. Not tarnish or degrade but lift them. That's what I found so interesting when I was able to examine the early German music centuries ago," he told me.

He toured with the Norman Luboff Choir and took a job writing jingles in an Omaha, NE advertising agency.

# CHIP DAVIS

He says he used to write on a 24-stave paper with a Scripto charcoal colored pencil. The ideas came a lot of time while playing the piano. "That's how I started. Now, I check it on Pro Tools. A lot of it I write in a stream of consciousness mode. I'm a classically trained musician and that's the way I thought. I go straight from my brain to the keyboard. I'll say 'Dave, get me a really cool percussion. I hear a really cool rhythm and I want to lay down a foundation.'"

*Chip Davis, founder of the multi platinum selling group Mannheim Steamroller* Photo by Scott Dobry

But he spent his early days making a living collaborating with friend Bill Fries writing music for a country western character C.W. McCall of 'Con- voy' fame. He co-wrote the number "Convoy." Earlier, the musical innovator joined with Jackson Berkey and Almeda Berkey to produce a series of creative environmental recordings about the seasons of the year called *Fresh Aire*.

The Berkeys re-joined Davis, all Christians, to produce and tour with a select group of musicians to play yuletide favorites called "Mannheim Christmas." Thanks to conservative talk show host Rush Limbaugh the CDs went viral. Within a few years, he was recording with Johnny Mathis and Olivia Newton-John. His electronic new age music continues to expand as the group (now two complete ensembles—red and green units) travel to more than 70 cities yearly at the holidays. As a friend in Syracuse, NY wrote me a year ago "It was a hoot! A great showcase for those who love the old hymns revived with modern ideas and rhythm. If today's pastors could listen with an open mind it would be a way to reach younger people."

In the 1990s, Chip launched Mannheim Steamroller's "An American Christmas," a 12-hour program nationally broadcasted to over 250 radio stations. It is distributed by WestStar Talk Radio.

In 2008, Chip was forced to leave the tour because of surgery but he continued planning and writing music to continue his venture.

"'Deck the Halls' was the first cut that I tackled in 1984 to do a Mannheim version of an existing Christmas carol," he wrote in the liner for a "Live Mannheim Concert" in Omaha, NE. "It turns out that 'Deck the Halls' is a Welch carol which works out good for me because the name Davis is a Welch name. So it kind of fell right that and I had a really great time."

He also excites his audiences with the sound of 16th century instruments.

To get the sound and flavor he wanted for "We Three Kings of Orient Are" he sought the necessary instruments. "I wanted to do a Mannheim version to help understand the instruments of the period like the dulcimer and dulcian. You might have imagined hearing this back in the ancient times when the three kings were riding on the camels."

Chip gets more enjoyment when his two daughters join him like they did on the haunting traditional carol, "Silent Night."

"To go out on stage with my two daughters my heart gets so big. Being out with my two girls and singing 'Silent Night' together... it's unbelievable to have raised them from babies. My eldest daughter, Kelly, works in our social media department. Along with my youngest daughter, Elyse, they are just incredible singers in their own right."

He's been a regular in the Macy's Thanksgiving Day Parade.

"It might not have happened," he told me. "That across –the – board skepticism only fueled my decision. For me, it was ok to tell people they were wrong about Christmas music. And today with more than 9 million copies sold I can look back and say 'well. We were right. You can successfully market Christmas music.'" He's probably getting closer to becoming the Billy Graham musically for the evangelical Christian movement.

Does he get requests from other bands wanting to play his music?

"Not that much anymore," he told Pollstar. He's located in Omaha, NE now and he loves larger gigs now. "I'm pretty hard to find. We have more mushrooms out here (Nebraska). They're an incredible taste treat. There's a short window of maybe two weeks when they grow. You cut them in half and then dunk them in egg and cracker crumbs and sauce and holy moley!"

What a way to write music! What a way to remain in a very difficult field.

Gert and I have seen four Mannheim Steamroller performances in New York and now in Florida. His creativity with centuries old music never fails to excite us. We'll be in his audience as long as he tours.

# Doobie Brothers

### The best of the Doobies: what a night!

My son-in-law Bob Middlebrook, a Miami Hurricane Marching Band drummer and graduate, handles security for major concerts along both Florida coasts these days and he comes up with great ways to get Gert and me involved. In 2015, he called us and said to get our dancing shoes on. "You're going to hear a great rock and roll group; get your wheelchair, Jack, and come down!"

The Doobie Brothers were at the Pompano Beach Amphitheater, South Florida, and he had tickets for us and we could go back stage to meet them. I had heard them several times before but I had no idea of the sound they produced. It was awesome! Thanks to my son, Bob, and several of his security people, I was back to experience what I thought I wanted to do in my life.

At a photo session back stage at the break, Pat Simmons, guitarist and one of the originals, spent most of the break telling me about the group and the people who made it all happen:

Son-in-law Bob Middle-brook who arranged my Doobie interview and others
Photo by Gert Behrens

"We've had a hardcore fan base here in Florida for years and they have handed down our music through the decades to their children and their children's children. I'd say that the band has still remained relevant musically though. I think the crowd would agree with me."

"I sometimes think the crowd knows our numbers as well as we do," he laughed. "Whether it's 'Listen to the music' or 'Black Water,' 'Jesus Is Alright' or 'China Grove' we're still getting played around the country 47 years later," he said.

"My songwriting is a little controlled and focused," he said, "I write with guitar---when I work on songs it comes from that marriage of ideas and playing guitar. I'm still old-school in that respect. We've always been more of a guitar band. Gotta remember, you always have to be aware of the traits that make people like you. I pay attention to that. If you're always trying to reinvent, you're trying too hard. You want to do what you do for the love of the music and for the pure enjoyment of doing it for people who love it. We're continuing the tradition."

Writer Rod Serling, who I interviewed years earlier, talked about

Doobie drummer, Ed Toth(left) with me at Florida concert  Photo by Gert Behrens

*The Doobies on stage at Pompano Beach, FL*
Photo by Gert Behrens

"time warp" and living in one. I really experienced the thrill that night, although confined to a wheelchair.

If you're over 65, I would suggest earplugs for those who want to try it. Otherwise, get as far as you can from the front of the stage.

Loud doesn't really describe it. Yet, it has some of the best guitar playing I've heard. Soft numbers, driven by a steady beat of frequently three drummers, three or more guitars and keyboard player, this is a group that forces your feet to move.

The Doobies became a force in modern music. Like Woody Herman, who introduced four saxophones, when he added a baritone saxophone to his "herd," it was innovative. The Herman band dedicated a number to it, called "Four Brothers."

That night at Pompano, guitarists John McFee, Pat Simmons and keyboardist, arranger, singer, composer Michael McDonald and back-up guitarists as well as drummers gave us a great evening of their music and received a number of enthusiastic encores.

Ask my wife Gert, not a groupie, but even she said she enjoyed the performance.

*John McFee, Doobie guitarist, and me back stage at Pompano, FL*
Photo by Gert Behrens

For those not familiar with the term "doobies" it came from the 1970s and refers to marijuana cigarettes which you rolled yourself. During my years with touring bands it was called "reefers." Believe it or not, I was still rolling corn silk into cigarettes then. Never joined the others. Corn silk tasted terrible and I gave it up...fast.

The Doobies are a different kind of musical "family" that over the years included a number of talented musicians. Among others they were: John Hartman, Tom Johnston, John Cowan, Guy Allison, Marc Russo, Tony Pia and lots of Californians (their base).

Think of the songs they introduced and it's like reminding yourself of the Beatles. It also reminds me of earlier bandleaders like Duke Ellington, Woody Herman, Stan Kenton, Ray Anthony, Claude Thornhill and so many of the bands who were around in the 1930s to 1980s when I was playing at ballrooms in various parts of Ohio, Pennsylvania, West Virginia, Michigan and Indiana. I spent long afternoons and evenings, for example, helping Stan Kenton drummers ---Stan Levey was one--- unload and set up a beautiful set of pearl rim drums and Zildjian cymbols.

Their creative sounds brought us songs like Minute By Minute, Keep This Train A-Rolling, One Step Closer, Real Life, The Doctor, You Belong To Me, China Grove, Black Water, Rockin' Down the Highway, Takin' It to the Streets and literally hundreds of other hits.

They began in San Jose, CA in 1970, and today they continue to tour as older members return and new members join the expanding family of Doobies. Typical of families, they feud, split up, regroup and continue to add new numbers to their vast portfolio of music that were very much California and their style.

Said one reviewer not long ago, "They are typical of a group of players but unique as a gathering of musicians having fun, arguing, very involved in their music and trying to create new hits."

The Doobies came at tumultuous time in American music history and they brought with them all kinds of followers from groupies to members of Hell's Angels and some found the Lord. They made it big time and lost it and continued to return. By the end of 1981, all of the originals had resigned and they were faced with starting all over again. The roar of the crowd and their own music and a tremendous data base of followers gave them rebirth after rebirth. It continues today. Reunion, follows reunion and their sound keeps resonating. Death has taken some of them.

Percussionists have suffered the most it seems. As any touring musician knows or learns quickly, road life seems exciting until you finish one year. So many young players see the gold too early in the tunnel. Broken marriages, bad health and the abject misery of loneliness on the road from one town to another has it's consequences along with bankruptcies, bad food and too much liquor and certainly too much smoking and drugs to stay awake until the next gig.

Read the obituaries of 1950 musicians like Stan Kenton, Claude Thornhill, Harry James and thousands of others and you get a dose of the reality that is behind the showbills. I've known a few in my life. Errol Garner, a talented, unschooled pianist told me after a gig "I've had so many of my good friends die alone and suffering. Yes, they came from good families as well as the street. They loved what they did but they died from it."

Some were Christians too. God loves talent but He has high standards regardless of your ability.

# TIM CONWAY

⭐⭐⭐⭐⭐

## Great run as a comic

Tim Conway and I were in the army together in the 1950's. He called our service time "Protecting our homeland from the Red Menace." We were both drafted in September 1956. We called it 'Harry Truman's Police Action." I never saw the Red Menace. I don't think Tim did either.

I saw North Koreans and the DMZ from the air and on the ground. I don't think Tim did. They were stone cold, cruel people. Their eyes told it all. Soldiers rarely spoke. Those assigned to military posts at Panmunjon's Freedom Village spoke excellent English, when they talked. But that wasn't often.

I was shoved off a stone walkway by a guard with a rifle butt in my back one day. He put his finger on the trigger and held it there for what seemed an eternity. Nobody stopped him. Our guards several feet away stood motionless. Then the North Korean laughed and walked back to his post. That tension goes on daily. I picked up the papers I was carrying and got myself up and continued on. I was furious but we had been warned not to provoke an incident. Out of the side of my eye I could see a smile forming on his face. Nobody said anything. Later, one of our guards told me that I had acted "appropriately." I responded "he was a little shit and I don't like to take such treatment." He said "get used to it here."

Tim, meanwhile, was doing some club work and television shows in the Cleveland area at the time. Of course, he later worked with Steve Allen, Carol Burnett and won four Emmy Awards on the way.

I was frantically finishing my final course work at Penn State on a Master's degree in American history and journalism. The Fairfield County, Ohio Selective Service Board had given me a summer term to complete but Penn State withdrew my scholarship. It was decided that because I had returned to my native state of Ohio, I was no longer eligible for a Pennsylvania scholarship.

It wax a rough time since Patty (my first wife) and I had married in June, just two weeks before I received my induction notice and the draft board moved the date of my departure to August the same year. We were living on a wedding gift check given us and more odds than ends. I noted a checkbook balance of six dollars a week before I was drafted.

Tim and I had graduated from Bowling Green State within a couple years of one another and we hadn't seen each other since . We met again later back stage at the Eastman Theater in Rochester, NY where he and Harvey Korman were doing a two person show (one of many they did before Harvey died). My son, Mark, got us tickets to see it and go backstage to meet the two comedians. Tim was the same as I remember him from college days. Very nonchalant and low key.

## TIM CONWAY

Trying to recall who I was, he looked at me and said "Oh, yes, Jack is it? "Glad to see you got back from Korea. We didn't graduate together did we?" Tim claimed he was at BG 11 years which made his bachelor's the most expensive state college four-year degree on record, I think. But that was Tim!

In his book *What's So Funny?* With Jane Scovell, who co-authored ElizabethTaylor and Ginger Rogers memoirs, he didn't discuss what I remember during our service years. My recall is excellent as my wife and doctors attested to years after I left the service. To remember details from Korea 60 years later is better than the Spanish I was forced to cram to pass for a second language requirement that I had forgotten just before I finished graduate work at Penn State. It was zany, nutty really. It happened!

Me, Tim Conway back stage at the Eastman Theatre in Rochester, NY where Harvey Korman and Tim were performing                                     Jack Behrens' Photo

Our experiences together with a number of other draftees in a huge repro depot in Fort Lewis could have brought criminal charges I felt. I mentioned it several times to Tim but got no answer. He was too busy planning the next escape from Army discipline .

He was especially good at impersonating southern career officers by words and drawl. "Yessir, captain, these here mens are with me to clean up this here area," he replied smartly and received a reassured salute from a dumbfounded motor pool officer. Tim got that comical smirk on his face and we were on our way in a US Army jeep he had no authority to have, or use for that matter.

There was a collective sigh of relief from five privates squeezed in the jeep. He put the vehicle in reverse and we lurched backward and nearly hit the startled officer. "Never will get these gears right!" he said as we careened forward finally in the right direction. That was Tim.

Those who have been placed in such camps for relocation know the idleness, the homesickness and the utter waste of time such hours are like. Picking up cigarette butts, paper wrappers, beer cans, condoms and a variety of litter. During one other episode a short time later, Tim took his "detail" by jeep to a base theater. An MP patrol passed us slowly and came back. The large military patrolman driving it asked Tim to provide papers for our purpose after 9 p.m "What's yur problem, son?" Tim responded. He reached down under the seat and pulled out a group of papers laying loose on the floor, held them and then told the MP "These here mens are on special orders with me. See these?" It was dark and the officer didn't have a flashlight. He took them to the front and with his jeep's headlights he proceeded to look like he was scanning them. He wasn't reading them, he was watching Tim. After studying them briefly he told us to continue on "but I don't want to see this jeep or any of you in this area again!"

"You got it!" Tim said with a salute and added "Youse have a great night."

Tim was a master of improvision. Just recall his great performances on Carol Burnett's show and how he caused fellow entertainers like Carol, Harvey Korman, Vicki Lawrence and others to double over from laughter at his look and strange antics. That also was the Tim I remember.

I didn't see him again that fall, 1957, until we were called from out barracks to board ships bound for Korea. I was on the upper deck and while near-sighted I thought I saw my Ohio friend dragging a duffle bag trailing socks, underwear and other items as a sergeant pushed and literally dragged him up a gangplank on board another vessel. He had told us he had met a USO woman who had seen him perform and he wouldn't go to Korea. I was curious about such order changes but then in the military...anything can happens...and usually does! I don't know what followed our time in Repo Seattle but we did have fun thanks to a guy who made millions laugh for years on television.   Amazing how we both "fought the red menace."

*"To my close friend Jack "*

Before meeting up with Tim in Rochester, NY I saw him on stage in Utica, NY where he and Tom Poston were performing in "Just for Laughs," 1994-95. Tim was inducted with Harvey later in the Television Arts & Sciences Hall of Fame.

Harvey passed on, regrettably. Like all things in our world, time just keeps moving on and on and death trails us relentlessly.

I remember a scene later from their performance at the beautiful old Stanley Theater on Main Street in Utica, NY where I taught for nearly three decades. Harvey was delivering a baseball player's farewell speech as Tim with a watering can on his head was echoing his words and taking pauses to elaborate Korman's inflated thoughts of false praise. Korman brought laughs then and later in Rochester when he introduced his friend and partner by saying: "A lot of people find him funny. I don't particularly."

I told him I still had the photograph he sent me when I saw him with Steve Allen on TV. On it he wrote the heading "photos are $1.50." He sent me a reply. "Photos are now $5."

That was Tim . . . Bowling Green graduates don't die. They just fade away.

# Epilogue

## How did I create my 23rd or 24th book?

How did I create my 23rd or 24th book? Short term memory says 23rd. Long term memory says, 24. Long term recall has been golden to me as you've read. And it's been accurate.

I still can remember my Army active duty number: US52414273 issued in 1956, 61 years ago. I even tried to forget it. It just stays there.

God told me to do this. That's not a comedian's line or fake news …that's the truth. God talks to all of us, if we listen.

I did, later in my lfe. My sister Bev will tell you and she always tells the truth! She got the looks in the family. I got the rhythm, two beautiful, loving wives, a squirrelly cat named Cleo, two great children, Cindy and Mark, now adults and four terrific young people—David, Joy, Rick and Bob—from my second marriage, a brother in law Jim Hietikko (a 6'4" 250 tackle for Woody Hayes' Big Ten championship Buckeyes) who once got so mad he threatened to flatten me in the family base-

## EPILOGUE

ment. I challenged him to a boxing match ( I was 150 pounds with clothes), he nearly had a seizure laughing and fell down. I helped him up and he began laughing once more and fell down again! We became fast friends until his death.

The Lord also gave me a patient first wife Patty, who for 53 years put up with long weekends of my work and trips to interview people in distant places and gave me the solitude that honed my skill at writing. That's been my journey. I wouldn't trade it, hardships, anguish and disappointments for all the money in the world!

If all second marriages were like ours the good Lord would be pleased, I think. We married three times in one year! First, in my home church in New Hartford, NY with friends Ruth Guthman, one of the few woman elders in our Missouri Synod Church, and pastor Rich Mokry's wife Miriam as our witnesses .

I was a changed person, said a close friend, John Crossley of Clinton. "You're happier and Gert has given you a better life and future." Our wedding and honeymoon aboard ship the Southern Princess Cruise Line bound for Hawaii and a trip around the islands. It was the first wedding on the ship in years. Weddings were held at dockside and couples then boarded. That meant, in case you're interested, waiting for an actual marriage license from Bermuda ...three months later.

We enjoyed it although the weather was typical for Christmas in the southern Pacific. We were like young newlyweds and anxious to get our lives started again though not sure where it would take us. Our final wedding ceremony was with Gert's family and friends in Burlington, VT. I discovered the value of the larger family. My parents had two children. Gert and her first husband had four and her three sons and one daughter have added the feeling of family that I really didn't know.

# EPILOGUE

Gert has given me so much in what is really a short time. She is not only loving and caring, she has expanded my values and thoughts about who I am.

I became much oriented to my faith and trying to use what I believe I can do as a writer to help others because I saw how she expanded her love of children to become a Guardian Ad Litem and work with the young. Her love of life was infectious and God sent. My work in the newspaper field had started to harden my views and shape what I didn't want to become. A bitter person absorbed with anger. I had seen that. I had grown up with that...I recognize it.

She became and remains my love, life and energy along with my inspiration for those around us. I'm the most fortunate man I can think of. I'm happy. In this day and age that's a great feeling daily!

And I still look forward too if God decides I'm of use. Four intriguing pastors—Pastor Paul Joslyn, Pastor Richard Mokry and his wife, Miriam, of Trinity Lutheran Church, New Hartford, NY; and Pastors Russ Johnson and Cris Escher of Grace Lutheran Church Port St. Lucie, FL—have nourished my spiritual needs at times when I wasn't sure I had more time or energy to go on. It's been a "team" effort for a guy whose father and mother were convinced he would fail because he didn't follow his successful dad in a 100-year-old insurance agency started by his grandfather, John.

I've been blessed with brothers and sisters in laws and grandchildren (and great-grandchildren) and my dad's work ethic that produced more than 16,000 articles and assignments for approximately 1,000 magazines and syndicates during my 6 years coveriing Presidents Johnson, Clinton, Carter and Reagan and was a part of a press pool during President Obama's first term. I was assigned to either Camp David or the White House. I researched and wrote 24 books to complete my writing career during 65 years of writing for more than

## EPILOGUE

250 magazines and newspapers with loads of acquaintances like Alex Haley, Tim Conway, Bob Hope, Tom Clancy, award-winning cartoonist Bill Sanders, bandleaders Woody Herman, Vaughn Monroe, Duke Ellington, the great Doobie Brothers and the Christmas season favorite, Chip Davis, and the Manheim Steam Rollers, Gannett publisher Al Neuharth, authors James Michener, Jessica Mitford and Tom Clancy, a joyful Ringling Brothers Barnum & Bailey clown Harry Sinclair, President Syngman Rhee of South Korea, President Ronald Reagan, President Jimmy Carter, President Bill Clinton, President Lyndon Johnson, and others in this book.

I'm also blessed to have a longtime Christian friend, Steve Lisi, who has made this book possible. As my disease progressed in my body I wondered if I could handle the stresses of working, putting together notes and and recall of all that I've witnessed and done. The devil is in the details of writing.

Steve is a PhD in graphics and organization in my opinion. I used to sign such degrees but I know in my heart there is no one who truly deserves that parchment paper more than Steve. Incidentally, Tom Clancy agreed with my assessment. He was most impressed with the covers of my books.

*Book signing of American Music*    Jack Behrens' Photo

Check out my books on *Camp David, American Music Makers, The*

# EPILOGUE

*Big Band Days: A Memoir.*

And I wouldn't have made it through some agonizing days, nights and nightmarish hospital visits in the last couple of years without the excellent care of British trained nurse, Ann Gonzales and caregiver Saundra Graham and RN Harry Harrichain who looks for alligators every time he visits us. It was said by Hilary Clinton "It takes a village." I'm a witness to that.

*Nationally reconized author, John C Behrens, at booksigning for Typewriter Guerrillas*
Jack Behrens' Photo

One of my astute journalism students, Fran Allred from Huntington, WVA, told me once that it's people who make all of us who we are. Even who we become. I think I demonstrate the validity of her observation.

This book gives you a glimpse of the times and people of the 1950s, '60s, '70s and '80s as I remember them. I astonish my wife Gert and even gerontologist colleague, Dr. Ron Lucchino of Utica College with my long term recall.

One morning not long ago, I clearly saw and smelled Korea, felt the freezing cold of 30 below zero temperature and saw the bleak Quonset hut we slept in 30 miles from the DMZ. I can't explain it. Doctors are puzzled but unwilling to try explain it to me but there it is. Old age I think.

Yet, some memories haunt me too. Watching a Korean policeman beat a boy to death on the street corner in Seoul and being held back when I tried to stop him has continued to give me a terrible feeling of pain.

## EPILOGUE

Having a repro depo bunk mate in Camp Zama, Japan, a chaplain's assistant, confide to me that he was shacking up although a happily newlywed just before he arrived in Korea was another memory I'd like to forget.

He gave me a letter to mail to his wife in Texas the night before. Sunday morning we had gone to church together. He smiled matter-of-factly and told me it was important because "We write daily." The next morning, he was dead due to an overdose of sleeping pills.

I looked at his shrouded body as I waited for graves registration people to come to take the body and a duty officer tried to gather details. Those thoughts just don't leave you, I find.

In many ways, the service was like walking the streets at night. Nameless people pass and vanish.

It was a young man (Pete Hart, later CEO of MasterCard) who graduated from our hometown high school in Lancaster, OH who helped me start my second life with Gert. He introduced me to eHarmony which brought us together.

Three years ago, as Gert and I headed for a new home in Port St. Lucie I lost the use of my hands and legs (Parkinson's) and couldn't walk more than a few feet without falling. I couldn't write or sign a check!

Today? I'm God's work-in-progress. I write on the computer daily, play my drums Gert bought me to join a Praise Band in the Trinity Lutheran Church, Utica, NY. I learned how to walk again with a walker I dislike but can't be without. I had to learn the painful way by just getting up and trying and falling down. Several falls and a hospital visit showed me what overconfidence can do to demoralize you.

## EPILOGUE

Thanks to my son Mark and his good friend, Jason Derr, I have a website (www.writerjackweb.com) to express my views and stay in a world that scares me more than my 14 months in Korea.

I've been blessed by God to grow up in the Midwest; Southern Ohia, that's how it's pronounced in the rolling and beautiful Hocking Hills. Go visit Lancaster, OH. Lots of blacktop where there used to be plush green, well-trimmed lawns and beautiful Elm and Cherry trees that shaded me on my way to school. It has remained a wonderful and wholesome place to live. The most important reason? Friendly

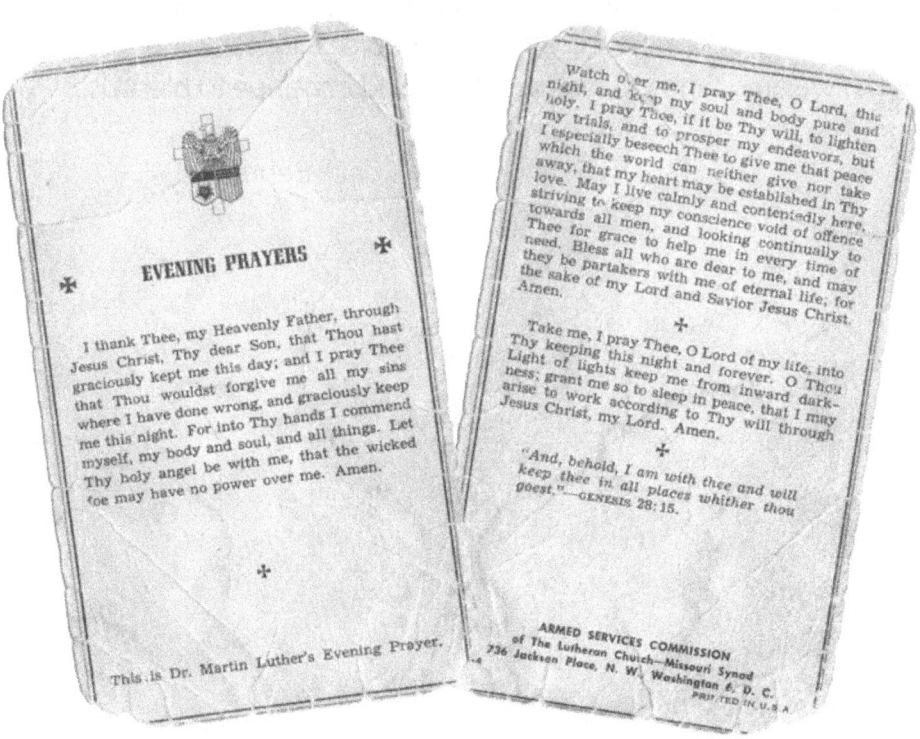

*My dog eared prayer card that was with me daily in Korea.*

people who welcome you with an honest sincerity that you remember long after you leave. I've lived in so many places where that's not the case although the signs entering the community tell you it's a "friendly town, village or city." But the Lancaster I left has always remained in my long term memory. It will be there when I leave.

That vivid recall also includes beautiful images of snow-capped Vermont where I met Gert, the luscious greenery of Huntington, West VA; the flatter but equally attractiveness of an old community in New York called Utica and a lovely village nearby, Clinton.

Port St. Lucie has its own unique charm as a relatively new city in Florida. It makes America the great country it is and my journey rich with stories of opportunity, sacrifice, choices, success and loss. That's what we are…and who we are. May God continue to bless us.

Jack Behrens

# TRIPLE WEDDING Celebration

In July of 2011 Jack and I had decided to marry, then planned a cruise ship wedding in December. We both had realized that life's too short, and didn't want to wait till December to share a home together, so we asked Jack's pastor in New Hartford, N.Y. to marry us in the eyes of the Lord, to honor His ways in marriage. In his comical way Pastor Rich asked, "Is this to be a shot-gun wedding?" That was July 6, 2011.

*Our 1st wedding on July 6, 2011 at Trinity Lutheran Church in New Hartford, NY with Rev. Richard Mokry officiating.*

We kept with our originally scheduled fairy tale ceremony on board the cruise ship, December 9, 2011.

Continuing with our year of weddings, at the request of my family, a third ceremony was officiated by my Pastor Jeff Jensen in my home church in Burlington, Vermont. Family was able to witness Jack and I, as we vowed to cherish each other on that Christmas Eve 2011. Pastor Jensen pronounced us as gifts to each other, and so we have remained each day of our lives together.

*2nd Wedding on board the Golden Princess on the way to Hawaii on Dec 9th 2011 with David Calabrese officiating.*

*3rd Wedding Dec 24th 2011 was at Community Lutheran Church in So. Burlington Vt. officiating Jeffry Jensen*

Captain Jack and his 32 foot Sea Ray cruiser on Oneida Lake, NY. Slept 6. I had been freelancing for 30 years and I had just signed a contract for my 20th book. To celebrate, I went to the bank to check my balance and was told that a change in policy allowed me to buy it on credit. I bought a 32' SeaRay on a Master card!

Jack and I with sister Beverly Hietikko

Jack and Gert with their first artificial tree in their Port St. Luce FL home (one of 7 Christmas trees in our house. Gert loves decorated trees!) We have the "Christmas home" in the neighborhood!

Jack and I dancing at my 80th birthday

www.ingramcontent.com/pod-product-compliance
Lightning Source LLC
Chambersburg PA
CBHW070937180426
43192CB00039B/2306